Contents

SAMS

Teach Yourself

Microsoft® Outlook™ 98

by Joe Habraken

in 10 Minutes

SAMS

A Division of Macmillan Computer Publishing
201 West 103rd St., Indianapolis, Indiana 46290 USA

To my grandmother, Kathryn, a truly wonderful person and the only person on the planet who still calls me Billy. I love you, Grandma.

International Standard Book Number: 0-672-31331-6

Library of Congress Catalog Card Number: 98-84762

00 99 8 7 6 5 4 3 2

Interpretation of the printing code: the rightmost double-digit number is the year of the book's first printing; the rightmost single-digit number is the number of the book's printing. For example, a printing code of 98-1 shows that this copy of the book was printed during the first printing of the book in 1998.

Screen reproductions in this book were created using Collage Plus from Inner Media, Inc., Hollis, NH.

Printed in the United States of America

Executive Editor Jim Minatel

Acquisitions Editor Jill Byus

Development Editor John W. Gosney

Technical Editor Kyle Bryant

Managing Editor Thomas F. Hayes

Project Editor Lori A. Lyons

Copy Editor Margaret Berson

Indexer Cheryl A. Jackson

Production Team Angela Calvert, Mary Hunt, Megan Wade

Introduction

Microsoft Outlook 98 is a personal information manager (PIM). With Outlook, you can communicate throughout your office or over the Internet with email, and you can also schedule meetings, create task lists for yourself and others, store documents in public folders that everyone can access, and launch Internet applications such as Microsoft Internet Explorer 4.1. Outlook provides accessibility and flexibility for you and your coworkers and friends.

The What and Why of Microsoft Outlook 98

Outlook can help you organize your work on a day-to-day basis. Using Microsoft Outlook, you can do the following:

- Create task lists
- Manage your calendar
- Log phone calls and other important events in your journal
- Make notes to remind yourself of important tasks

Additionally, Outlook can help you communicate with others and share your workload. When you and your coworkers use the combined features of Microsoft Outlook and Microsoft Office, you can:

- Schedule meetings and invite coworkers
- Communicate with others using email on your company's network and over the Internet
- Import and export files
- Share data and documents through public folders
- Communicate with others over the Internet

Microsoft Outlook is easy to learn and offers many advantages and benefits in return. This book can help you understand the possibilities awaiting you with Microsoft Outlook.

This book concentrates on using Outlook on a Windows 95/ Windows NT 4.0 workstation on which Microsoft Office is also installed. Note, however, that you will also be able to install Microsoft Outlook on a computer running Windows 98 and Windows NT 5.0, when these operating systems become available.

WHY *SAMS' TEACH YOURSELF MICROSOFT OUTLOOK 98 IN 10 MINUTES*?

Sams' Teach Yourself Microsoft Outlook 98 in 10 Minutes can save you precious time while you get to know the program. Each lesson is designed to be completed in 10 minutes or less, so you can master basic Outlook skills quickly.

Although you can jump around among lessons, starting at the beginning is a good plan. The bare-bones basics are covered first, and more advanced topics are covered later. If you need help installing Outlook, see the next section for instructions.

INSTALLING OUTLOOK

You can install Microsoft Outlook to a workstation running Windows 95 or Windows NT 4.0. (Outlook will *not* run on a computer running Windows for Workgroups, Windows 3.x, or Windows NT 3.5.) In addition, you can install Outlook in conjunction with Microsoft Office 97, or you can install just the Outlook program.

To install Outlook, follow these steps:

1. Start your computer. Insert the Microsoft Office or Outlook 98 CD in the CD-ROM drive.
2. Choose Start, Run. Alternatively, open the CD and choose the Setup icon.

CD May AutoPlay If you install Outlook 98 from a CD-ROM, the first time you place the CD-ROM in your CD drive you may find that the CD "autoplays" and takes you directly to the installation screen. If this is the case, you will not need to do steps 2 and 3 as outlined here.

3. In the Run dialog box, type the letter of the CD-ROM drive, followed by setup (for example, **e:\setup**). If necessary, use the Browse button to locate and select the CD-ROM drive and the setup.exe program.
4. When Setup prompts you, enter your name and organization. Then confirm that they are correct.
5. Choose either the Typical or the Custom option.
6. Follow the onscreen instructions to complete the installation.

Microsoft also offers software upgrades via their Web site. You can download Microsoft Outlook 98 if you already own Microsoft Outlook 97 or Microsoft Office 97. Go to **http://www.microsoft.com/outlook/**. Follow the directions on this Web page to locate the Outlook 98 download page.

When you reach the Outlook 98 download page, you can click the link that will begin the download process. Outlook 98 uses Microsoft's Active Setup—you will download a small installation program that you will then use to actually download and install Outlook. Make sure that you have the CD_key ready for your copy of Outlook or Office 97. You will be asked to provide this number to download the setup program (it's usually on the back of the jewel box that the software CD came in).

After you download the installation program, remain connected to your Internet Service provider. Locate the file you downloaded and double-click it. Outlook's Active Setup will begin. Follow the prompts provided by the Active Setup Wizard to download and install the new version of Outlook.

At the very beginning of the installation process, you will be asked if you want to install Outlook for Internet E-mail Only or Corporate E-mail (a third choice is available for no email). Lesson 3 of this book discusses the effect that these two different installations have on Outlook functionality. You may want to review Lesson 3 briefly before selecting your installation.

CONVENTIONS USED IN THIS BOOK

To help you move through the lessons easily, these conventions are used:

Onscreen text	Onscreen text appears in bold type.
Text you should type	Information you need to type appears in bold colored type.
Items you select	Commands, options, and icons you are to select and keys you are to press appear in colored type.

In telling you to choose menu commands, this book uses the format *menu title, menu command*. For example, the statement "choose File, Properties" means to "open the File menu and select the Properties command."

In addition, *Sams' Teach Yourself Microsoft Outlook 98 in 10 Minutes* uses the following icons to identify helpful information:

Plain English New or unfamiliar terms are defined in (you got it) "plain English."

Timesaver Tips Read these tips for ideas that cut corners and confusion.

Panic Button This icon identifies areas where new users often run into trouble; these tips offer practical solutions to those problems.

ACKNOWLEDGMENTS

Creating books like this takes a real team effort. I would like to thank Jill Byus, our acquisitions editor, who worked very hard to assemble the team that made this book a reality. I would also like to thank John Gosney, who served as the developmental editor for this book and who came up with many great ideas for improving the content of the book. Also a tip of the hat and a thanks to Kyle Bryant, who as the technical editor for the project did a fantastic job making sure that everything was correct and suggested a number of additions that made the book even more technically sound. Finally, thanks to our editors, Margaret Berson and Lori Lyons, who ran the last leg of the race and made sure that the book made it to press on time—what a great team of professionals.

TRADEMARKS

COMMENTS AND SUGGESTIONS

We want you to let us know what you like or dislike most about this book or other Sams products. Your comments will help us to continue publishing the best books available on computer topics in today's market.

Publisher
Sams Publishing
201 West 103rd Street
Indianapolis, Indiana 46290 USA

To order other Sams or Macmillan Computer Publishing books, catalogs, or products, please contact our Customer Service Department at **800/858-7674** or fax us at **800/835-3202** (International Fax: 317/228-4400). Or visit our online bookstore at **http://www.mcp.com/**.

LESSON 1

What's New in Outlook 98

In this lesson, you are introduced to Outlook's powerful organizing features, and you learn what's new in Outlook 98.

Getting Organized with Outlook 98

Outlook 98 is the latest version of Microsoft's popular personal information manager (PIM). Outlook can help you manage incoming and outgoing messages, such as email and faxes, and help you keep organized by providing a personal calendar, a contacts list, and a personal to-do list.

Personal Information Manager (PIM) A PIM is a software package that helps you keep track of your appointments, meetings, contacts, and messages, such as email and faxes.

Outlook 98 also makes it easy for you to quickly connect to the Internet via Microsoft's powerful Web browser, Internet Explorer 4. You can even use Outlook to connect to an online, real-time meeting using Microsoft NetMeeting, which can provide video and audio conferencing with one or more participants.

Outlook's ultimate purpose is to keep you organized. Its basic "look and feel" is designed to help you as you work with messages, contacts, lists, and appointments.

When you install Outlook 98, Microsoft's Internet Explorer 4.0 is also installed. It is considered an essential part of your Outlook 98 configuration. Internet Explorer 4.0 will replace your current version of Internet Explorer.

Outlook 98 is completely compatible with Microsoft Office 97. However, you cannot have more than one version of Outlook installed on your computer. So, when you install Outlook 98, it will replace Outlook 97. You will also find that Outlook 98 adds some new features to your Microsoft Office installation. For example, when you open a file in an Office application, an animated folder appears during the process. Outlook 98 also adds an additional Office Assistant for your use—Virgil the cat.

OUTLOOK FOLDERS

Outlook provides an environment that's very much like a filing cabinet. Items of information are kept in folders, which you can access with one click of the mouse. For instance, your new email and fax messages can be found in the Inbox. Appointments, meetings, and events are stored in the Calendar folder. Contacts—their email addresses, business addresses, fax numbers, and phone numbers—are stored in the Contacts folder.

Folders are also available for your Tasks, Journal Entries, and Notes. Outlook also keeps track of your Deleted Items and Sent Items in folders. Outlook 98 also has a new feature called Net Folders. These folders allow you to share Outlook information with others over the Internet or a corporate intranet. Any Outlook item, such as messages, tasks, or appointments, can be shared using these special folders.

OUTLOOK CATEGORIES

Outlook enables you to fine-tune the organization of the information in your various folders by assigning items to categories. For instance, you may want to categorize a particular meeting that you've attended or notes that you've recorded as being related to your most important customers. Outlook provides a Key Customer category. After you designate items in the Key Customer category, you can then easily find them or group them, no matter which folder they reside in. A grouping of items for the Key Customer category may include email messages, faxes, appointments, contacts, or notes.

Outlook provides a number of ready-made categories such as Key Customer, Ideas, Hot Contacts, and Strategies. You can also create your own categories or delete categories that you no longer need.

NEW FEATURES IN OUTLOOK 98

Outlook 98 contains a number of improvements that make it even easier for you to stay on top of the information that you keep in your various folders. New features have also been added that make Outlook 98 much more "Internet ready" than the previous version.

THE OUTLOOK SETUP WIZARD

The new Setup Wizard gives you the option of configuring Outlook for either Internet email only or a corporate email account (see Figure 1.1). Outlook 98 also provides you with the capability to send and receive faxes, whether you choose to use Internet email or the corporate email settings.

The Setup Wizard can also import existing email accounts from other email clients like Outlook Express, Netscape Messenger, or Eudora mail. If you've used a previous version of Outlook, the Setup Wizard can also import existing accounts, profiles, folders, and personal address books.

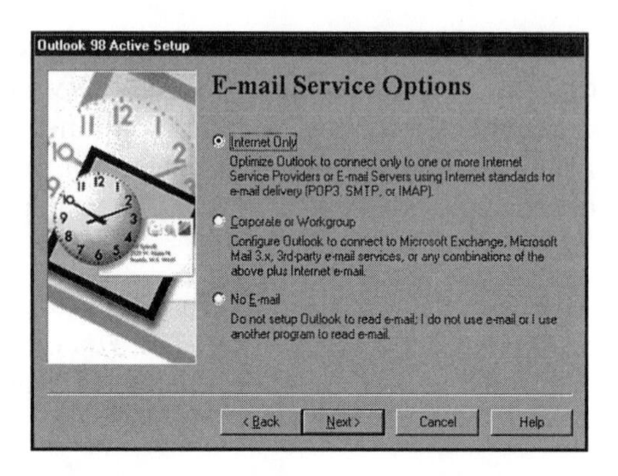

FIGURE 1.1 The Outlook Setup Wizard helps you select the type of email account you want to use.

Connection Choices The Internet Only selection means that you will send and receive email over the Internet by connecting with a modem to an Internet service provider. If you are connected to a corporate network or if you dial in to a corporate network using your modem, the best choice for you is the Corporate or Workgroup setting. This selection still allows you to send Internet email.

What If I Use America Online? If you use America Online, you will not be able to use Outlook 98 as your email client. However, you can still use all the other features that Outlook offers.

THE RULES WIZARD AND ORGANIZER TOOL

The new Rules Wizard and Organizer tool are two features that help you create rules that can forward, move, delete, or flag incoming and outgoing email. For instance, you may want all email from a certain sender to be transferred to a special folder. Important email that you want to forward to other individuals can also be handled automatically.

Rules created using the Rules Wizard can be based on the sender of the message or the content of the message. You can create a rule that will categorize messages with a certain content. Or you can flag messages received from a particular person.

The Organize tool provides an easy-to-use interface that allows you to quickly organize your message using folders, colors, flags, and special views. It also helps you create simple rules to organize messages from a particular person. Most importantly, it can help you create rules that quickly deal with nuisance messages that you consider "junk mail."

Outlook Today

Outlook provides you with a new tool—Outlook Today—that enables you to check all the items, such as appointments, meetings, tasks, and new email, for the current day. The Outlook Today window (see Figure 1.2) also enables you to look up a particular person in any of your contact or address books using a fast and easy search engine.

You can customize the Outlook Today screen to show your Calendar items for more than one day and even have it provide you with a list of all your active tasks. Outlook Today can be customized so that Outlook automatically opens it when you start the software, giving you the ability to always stay up-to-date on your schedule and new messages.

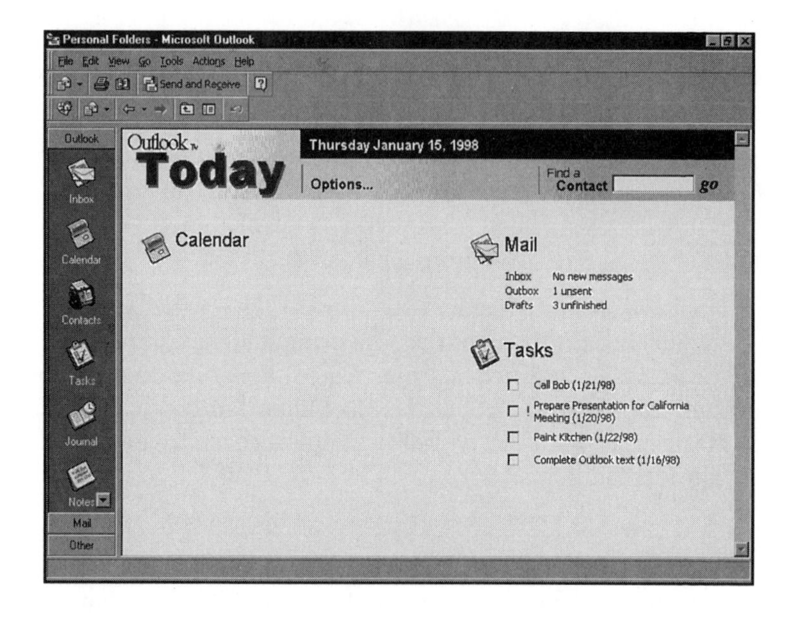

FIGURE 1.2 The Outlook Today window shows you all the appointments, tasks, and new email for the day.

OUTLOOK AND INTERNET EXPLORER 4

Outlook 98 is seamlessly integrated with the components of Microsoft's Internet Explorer 4 so that you can quickly access an important World Wide Web page, read Usenet newsgroup postings, or launch an online meeting using Microsoft NetMeeting. Outlook can also be configured as your default email client so that it opens when you click a Web page email link in the Internet Explorer window.

When Outlook 98 is installed, Internet Explorer 4 and the Outlook Express NewsReader are also installed. Microsoft NetMeeting can be downloaded as an addition to your Internet Explorer 4 configuration at **http://www.microsoft.com/ie4** or from the NetMeeting Web page at **http://www.microsoft.com/netmeeting/**.

OTHER USEFUL FEATURES

Outlook 98 also provides several other features that make it easier for you to stay organized. These new features range from a preview pane for your messages to the ability to recall messages that you've sent.

- **AutoPreview and Preview Pane** These two new features make it easy for you to preview and read your email messages. AutoPreview provides a view of your email messages that includes the first three lines of the message. The Preview Pane displays the entire contents of the message, so that you don't have to open a separate window.
- **Message Recall** This feature allows you to recall any sent message as long as the recipient has not opened it. You can also replace a sent message with a newer, updated message using this feature. Message Recall is only supported on networks using Microsoft Exchange Server. This particular feature will not allow you to recall messages over the Internet.
- **Contact Manager** You can use this feature to dial a phone call with a particular contact, send email to a specific recipient, or set up an online meeting using Microsoft NetMeeting. You can even use this feature to download a map of a contact's address using Microsoft Expedia's Web-based travel service.

Exploring New Features This book will give you a chance to explore each of the new Outlook 98 features previewed in this chapter.

In this lesson, you learned how Outlook can help you stay organized. You were also introduced to some of the new features found in Outlook 98. In the next lesson, you will take a first look at the Outlook window and learn how to start and exit the software. You will also learn how to use the mouse to navigate through the various features of the program.

LESSON 2

Navigating Outlook

In this lesson, you learn to start and exit Outlook, identify parts of the Outlook window, and use the mouse to get around the program.

Starting Outlook

You start Outlook from the Windows desktop. After starting the program, you can leave it open, or you can minimize it to free up the desktop for other applications. Either way, you can access it at any time during your work day.

Outlook and System Performance If you leave Outlook open on your desktop, it will still require a certain amount of your system resources. This means that if you normally run multiple applications such as Word and Excel, you may see some loss of performance as you work. If this becomes a problem, close Outlook to free up your system's memory.

To start Microsoft Outlook, follow these steps:

1. From the Windows desktop, click the Start button and choose Programs, Microsoft Outlook. (If you have customized your Start menu, Outlook may appear within a folder, such as a Microsoft Office folder on the Programs menu.) You can also double-click the Outlook shortcut icon on the desktop to start Outlook.
2. If the Choose Profile dialog box appears, click OK to accept the default profile or choose your profile and open Microsoft Outlook. Figure 2.1 shows the Outlook screen that appears.

Use the Office Toolbar You can also launch Outlook from the Office toolbar if it is present on your desktop. Click the Office menu button to add the Outlook button to the Office toolbar.

Profile Information about you and your communication services that is created automatically when you install Outlook. The profile includes your name, user ID, post office, and so on. Additional profiles allow you to set up Outlook for more than one user or a different set of communication services. Configuration issues regarding Outlook and Internet Mail Only and Corporate E-mail will be addressed in more detail in Lesson 3, "Understanding the Outlook Configuration."

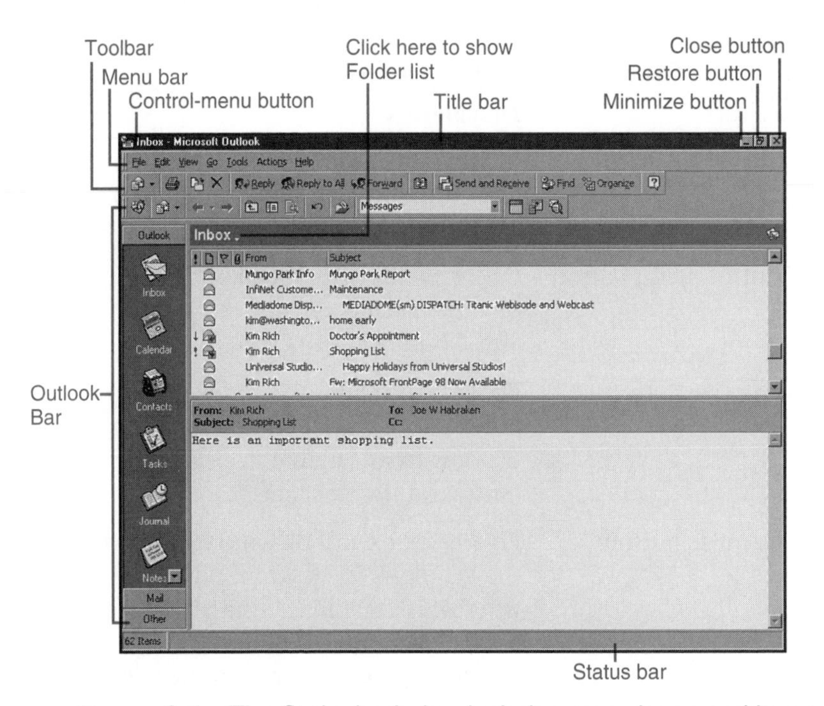

FIGURE 2.1 The Outlook window includes many icons and items you'll use in your daily routine.

UNDERSTANDING THE OUTLOOK WINDOW

The Outlook Window includes items you can use to navigate and operate the program. If you do not see some of the items listed in Figure 2.1 on your screen, open the View menu and select the command for the appropriate element (such as Toolbars, Status Bar, Folder List, or Outlook Bar). A check mark in front of an item means the item is currently showing.

Close the Preview Pane If you find the Preview Pane distracting when you first open the Outlook Window, click the View menu and click Preview Pane (removing the check mark) to close the Preview Pane.

Table 2.1 describes the elements you see in the opening screen.

TABLE 2.1 ELEMENTS OF THE OUTLOOK WINDOW

ELEMENT	DESCRIPTION
Title bar	Includes the name of the application and current folder, plus the Minimize, Maximize, and Close buttons.
Control-menu button	Opens the Control menu, which provides such commands as Move, Size, Minimize, and Close.
Minimize button	Reduces the Outlook window to a button on the taskbar; to restore the window to its original size, click the button on the taskbar.
Maximize button	Enlarges the Outlook window to cover the Windows 95 desktop. When the window is maximized, the Maximize button changes to a Restore button that you can click to return the window to its previous size.

ELEMENT	DESCRIPTION
Close (X) button	Closes the Outlook program.
Menu bar	Contains menus of commands you can use to perform tasks in the program.
Toolbar	Includes icons that serve as shortcuts for common commands, such as creating a new message or printing a message.
Show Folder list	Displays the current folder. Click this to display a list of Personal Folders you can open.
Outlook Bar	Displays icons representing folders: Inbox, Calendar, Contacts, and so on. Click an icon to change to the folder it names. The Outlook, Mail, and Other buttons on the bar list specific groups of folders (for instance, the Mail button lists icons related to your mail, such as the Inbox and Sent items).
Status bar	Displays information about the items currently shown in the Information Viewer.
Preview Pane	Displays a preview of the currently selected item in your Outlook Inbox or other selected folder.
Office Assistant	The Office Assistant provides you with the help you need to get the most out of Outlook. Click the Assistant when you need help.

Finding a Toolbar Button's Purpose You can place the mouse pointer on any toolbar button to view a description of that tool's function.

USING THE MOUSE IN OUTLOOK

As with most Windows-based programs, you can use the mouse in Outlook to select items, open mail and folders, move items, and so on. In general, clicking selects an item, and double-clicking selects it *and* performs some action on it (for example, displaying its contents).

- In addition to clicking and double-clicking, there are some special mouse actions you can use in Outlook. First, to move an object to another position on the screen (to transfer a mail message to another folder, for example), you can *drag* the object with the mouse. To drag an objecs«(õ a new location onscreen, point to the object and press and hold down the left mouse button. Move the mouse pointer to the new location, and then release the mouse button.
- As another example, you can display a shortcut menu by clicking the right mouse button when pointing to an item. For instance, you can right-click a folder in the Outlook Bar or a piece of mail. A shortcut menu appears, which usually contains common commands relating to that particular item.
- Finally, you can act upon multiple items at once by selecting them before issuing a command. To select multiple contiguous items, hold down the Shift key and click the first and last items you want to select. To select noncontiguous items (those that are not adjacent to each other), hold down the Ctrl key and click each item.

If You Prefer the Keyboard You can use the keyboard to move around Outlook and to access many, but not all, of its features. For example, to open a menu with the keyboard, press the Alt key and then press the underlined letter in the menu name (press Alt+F to open the File menu, for instance). This book concentrates on using the mouse to perform tasks in Outlook; however, some keyboard shortcuts are included in tips along the way.

EXITING OUTLOOK

When you're finished with Outlook, you can close the program in several different ways:

- Choose File, Exit (to remain connected to the mail program).
- Choose File, Exit and Log Off (to disconnect from the mail program).
- Double-click the application's Control-menu button.
- Click the application's Control-menu button and choose Close from the menu.
- Press Alt+F4.
- Click the Close (X) button at the right end of Outlook's title bar.

DO I NEED TO LOG OFF?

If you are connected to your email service through your corporate network, you really do not need to log off or close Outlook. This allows Outlook to periodically check the mail server for new mail. When you log off your corporate network and close down your computer, your connection to the mail server is also shut down. New email will wait for you on the server and be downloaded the next time you log on to the network and start Outlook.

If you receive your email through a mail server run by an Internet service provider, you connect through a dial-up connection. After you download your email from the server using Outlook, you may want to disconnect from your provider to save on connection time or to free up your phone line. Figure 2.2 shows the connection box used for a dial-up service. To close the connection, click Disconnect.

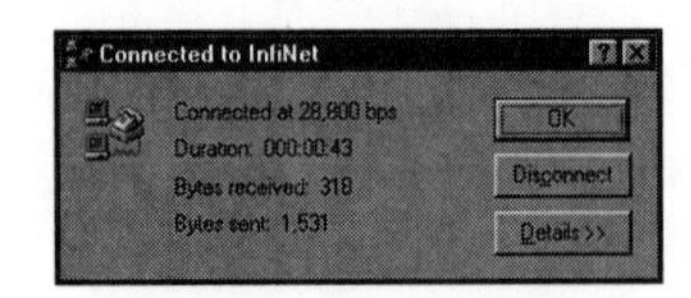

FIGURE 2.2 After downloading your email from your Internet service provider, you may want to close the connection.

In this lesson, you learned about the Outlook window, how to start and exit Outlook, and how to use the mouse to get around the program. In the next lesson, you will learn to open menus, select commands, and use dialog boxes and the toolbar.

LESSON 3

Understanding the Outlook Configurations

In this lesson, you learn how to set up Outlook for Internet Only or Corporate email and how to configure these two different options.

Choosing Your Outlook Installation

The choices that you make during Outlook's initial installation will affect the functionality of the Outlook software and the features that are available to you. Don't be overly concerned with the preceding statement; you can reinstall components of Outlook at any time or change your installation depending on your needs.

Outlook 98 really comes in two flavors: Internet Only and Corporate (or WorkGroup) email service. Which configuration you choose really revolves around whether you are connected to a corporate network or using Outlook as your Internet email client. Each installation also has certain ways of handling the sending and receiving of messages, the handling of faxes, and how collaboration with other users is conducted.

Installation Considerations

When you begin the Outlook 98 installation, you should be aware that any previous version of Outlook will be replaced. Another inescapable result of the Outlook 98 installation is that Internet Explorer 4.01 (or later version) will be installed replacing any previous versions of Microsoft Internet Explorer that you have on your computer. You don't have to use Internet Explorer 4.01 as your default Web browser, but it must be installed on the computer for Outlook to have full functionality.

Really the only major installation decision that you must make is whether you want Internet Only email, Corporate email, or no email at all, as shown in Figure 3.1. The following sections look at the first two possibilities separately.

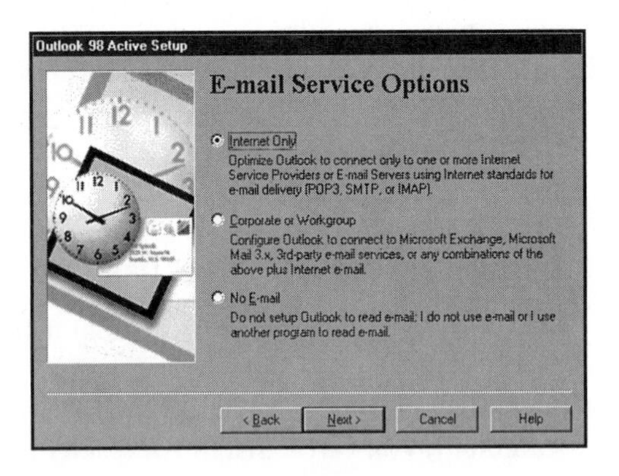

FIGURE 3.1 You must select the type of electronic mail you will use with Outlook.

INTERNET ONLY EMAIL

If you select Internet Only email, this could mean either of two things: you connect to the Internet using a modem and an Internet Service Provider (ISP); or you are physically connected to a network at your place of business, but your company does not operate a special network mail server with Microsoft Exchange Server software installed on it or another corporate email server software package installed on it. Basically your company's network is just a conduit to the Internet, just as your modem is at home.

This means that your sending and receiving of email will use Internet Protocols such as POP3 and SMTP.

ISP (Internet Service Provider) A commercial, educational, or government institution that provides individuals and companies access to the Internet.

POP3 (Post Office Protocol version 3) A set of rules used to download mail to your computer. Your ISP uses a POP3 host, or server, to get your mail to you.

SMTP (Simple Mail Transfer Protocol) A set of rules used to transfer Internet mail; your ISP goes through an SMTP host, or relay, server to get your mail to you.

The only features in Outlook that will be affected by your selection of Internet Only email will be your mail service and your fax service. The Calendar, Contacts, Notes, and Tasks features will operate the same. However, the way that you share Calendar and Contacts information with other users will be different than it would be on a corporate network using Exchange Server.

This issue of Internet Only or Corporate installation may be further confused if your corporation has adopted the connectivity strategy called *intranet*. An intranet uses the Internet protocols such as POP3/SMTP email rather than other proprietary systems such as Microsoft Mail. Check with your network administrator before installing Outlook in the workplace.

One other point concerning the two different email configurations in Outlook is the different formats that are available to you for sending mail. The Internet Only configuration allows you to send messages as Text Only and Rich Text (HTML). The Rich Text (HTML) format for the Internet Only configuration is really just HTML, so do not be confused by the Rich Text reference. When you send HTML messages, you can use special fonts, bold, underline, and other font attributes. If the person receiving the message has an email client that can read HTML, that person will see your special formatting.

The Corporate configuration provides you with the Text Only format and the Rich Text (HTML) format and adds a third format,

Rich Text Format (RTF). This Rich Text Format is normally used for messages sent locally on your corporate network. Local mail networks at a company usually employ the same email client, so each user can take advantage of this RTF format. This RTF format differs from the RTF (HTML) format because it is particular to proprietary email packages, such as Microsoft Mail, and was not really designed to be used for messages sent over the Internet. The term *Rich Text* really refers (in both the HTML and Rich Text formats) to the fact that the text in the message can be formatted using special text attributes such as bold, underline, and italic.

CONFIGURING AN INTERNET EMAIL ACCOUNT

When you start Outlook for the first time after the installation in which you chose Internet Only, you will be asked to configure your Internet email account. If your previous version of Outlook (or other Internet email client, such as Outlook Express) was configured for an Internet email account, this information is imported into Outlook 98 during the installation process (a screen during preinstallation asks you to select the email client that you want to import the information from).

If no previous configuration exists, the Internet Connection Wizard will walk you through the process of creating an Internet email account as shown in Figure 3.2.

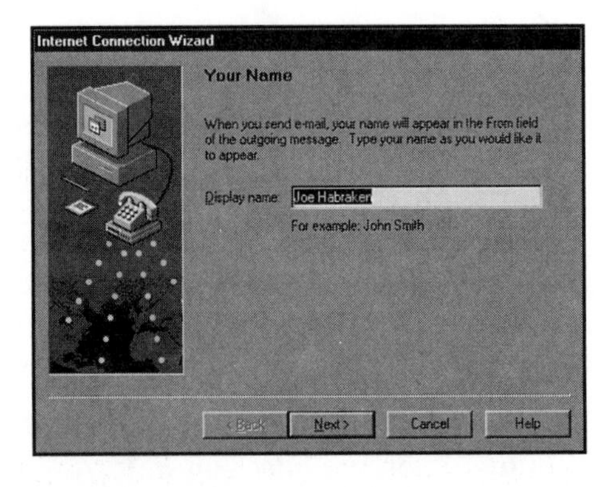

FIGURE 3.2 The Internet Connection Wizard helps you configure your Internet email account.

Install It Any Time You can install your Internet email account at any time using the Connection Wizard. Click Tools, Accounts. In the Accounts dialog box Mail tab, click Add, and then select Mail.

The Internet Connection Wizard will ask you to provide your name, your Internet email account address (probably **yourname@ company.com**), and the names of your POP3 Server (for incoming mail) and your SMTP Server (for outgoing mail). You need to get this information from your ISP or Network Administrator.

You will also be asked your POP account name and password. This information, again, must be provided to you by your ISP or Network Administrator.

The Internet Connection Wizard will also ask you to provide a "friendly" name for the account you are creating. This is the name that will appear in the Outlook Services box.

The final step in the Internet email configuration is to select the way that you will connect to the Internet. You can connect using your phone line (Outlook will help you make the connection each time you send mail), or connect using your corporate network as shown in Figure 3.3. A third choice is available if you want to manually connect to the Internet before attempting to send or receive mail using Outlook.

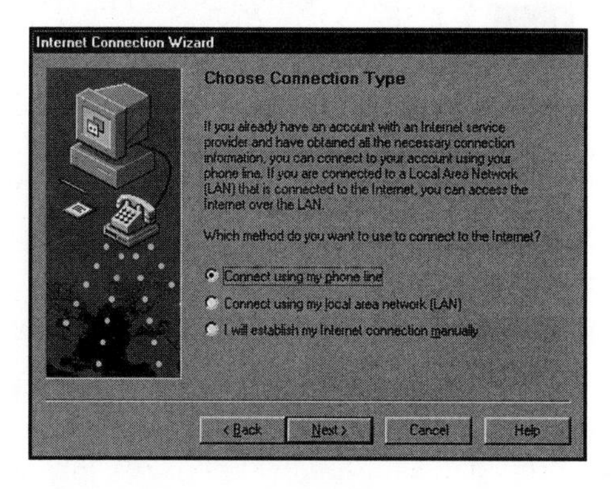

FIGURE 3.3 Choose how you will connect to the Internet when you send and receive messages using your email account.

The final step in the process asks you to select an existing dial-up connection or create a new one to connect to the Internet (if you chose the Connect Using Your Phone Line option in the previous step).

Dial-up connections dial the phone number of your service provider and connect you to their Internet server using your modem. If you configure a new dial-up connection, you must know your username, password, and the phone number for your ISP's Internet server.

Dial-Up Networking You must have the Windows 95 or NT Dial-Up Networking protocol installed to create new dial-up connections. See your operating system documentation to learn how to configure the Windows dial-up adapter.

After you configure your Internet email account, you are ready to send and receive messages.

Configuring Internet Only Fax Support

Outlook 98 also allows you to send and receive faxes. If you configure Outlook for Internet Only and choose to send and receive faxes, Outlook Fax will be installed. Outlook Fax can send faxes over your modem and answer your phone to receive incoming faxes.

The Outlook Fax service is automatically installed during the initial installation of Outlook (if you choose Internet Only fax support during installation) and will appear as one of the accounts in the Accounts dialog box.

Sharing Information on the Internet

Even if you are not connected to a corporate network that uses Microsoft Exchange Server to share Outlook folder information, you can share your Calendar and Contacts information with others by means of the Internet. Outlook 98 contains a feature called Net Folders. These special folders allow you to share information on the Internet with anyone you can send Internet email to.

CORPORATE EMAIL

If you select the Corporate email configuration for Outlook during the installation process, chances are that you will be using Outlook as a corporate email client over your company's network. If your company has a Microsoft Exchange server on the network, you will be using Outlook in an ideal environment.

CONFIGURING YOUR EMAIL ACCOUNT

If you use corporate email, your network administrator will provide you with a mail account. You may or may not be allowed to choose your own user name and password for the account. Your corporate email account will be configured as an account that appears in the Account dialog box. Using the Corporate email configuration allows you to take advantage of Outlook features such as the message recall, where you can recall a mail message that has not been opened by the recipient.

If you also desire to send and receive Internet email using the corporate configuration, you must also create an Internet email account. You can do this by using the Internet Connection Wizard discussed earlier in the chapter.

SHARING INFORMATION

Working on a corporate network that uses Exchange Server enables you to publish contact lists or calendars to a Microsoft Exchange Server public folder. Collaboration is made easy in the Exchange Server environment, and when you use Outlook to schedule a meeting, the availability of all the participants can be checked and routed to you immediately. A number of third-party collaboration applications also exist, making the Exchange Server environment ideal for employees using Outlook as their collaboration client.

Using Outlook on an Exchange Server network enables a number of email features not available in the Internet Only email configuration. On a network, you can redirect replies, set message expirations, and even grant privileges to other users to monitor your email, calendar, contacts, and tasks.

Working on a corporate network also enhances your ability to share information between users. Any folder on your computer can be set up as a shared resource.

Another plus of working on a network is that you can stay connected to the network throughout the day. There need be no concern over connect time as there is with an Internet dial-in account. Being connected to the network constantly not only means that corporate email will be downloaded to your computer periodically, but also that any incoming Internet email will also be downloaded throughout the day.

Using Net Folders on a Corporate Network If you are on a corporate network, you can still take advantage of Net Folders to share information with people over the Internet.

In this lesson, you learned about the Internet Only and the Corporate email configurations for Outlook 98. In the next lesson, you will learn the various Outlook tools such as the Outlook Bar.

Using Outlook's Tools

In this lesson, you learn to change views in Outlook, use the Outlook Bar, and use the folder list.

Using the Outlook Bar

Each Outlook organization tool has its own folder. You have a folder for email (Inbox), a folder for the calendar (Calendar), and so on. The Outlook Bar is a tool you can use to quickly change folders in Outlook. The icons in the Outlook Bar represent all of the folders available to you and provide shortcuts to getting to the contents of those folders. Figure 4.1 shows the Outlook Bar.

Three groups are located within the Outlook Bar: Outlook, Mail, and Other. Each group contains related folders in which you can work.

- **The Outlook group** contains folders for working with the different organizational tools in Outlook, such as the Inbox, Calendar, Tasks, and so on.
- **The Mail group** contains folders for organizing and managing your electronic mail and faxes.
- **The Other group** contains folders on your computer, such as My Computer and My Documents, and you can use it to work with files and folders outside Outlook. To switch from one group to another, click the Outlook, Mail, or Other button in the Outlook Bar. The Outlook group is displayed by default.

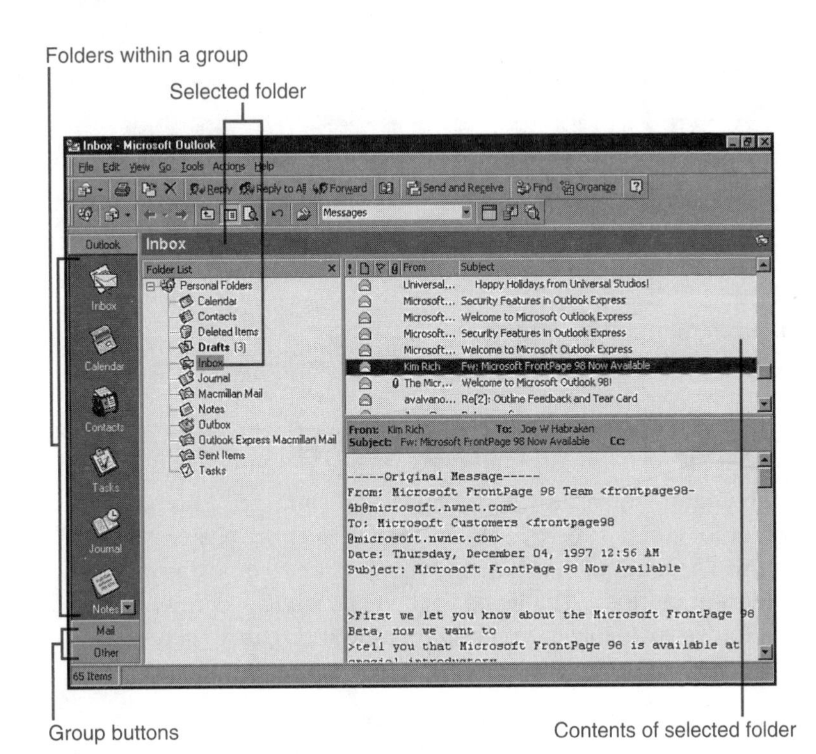

FIGURE 4.1 Use the Outlook Bar to view various items in your work.

THE OUTLOOK GROUP FOLDERS

The Outlook group's folder icons in the Outlook Bar enable you to access your work in Outlook. That includes your mail messages, appointments, address list, and so on. Table 4.1 describes each of the folders within the Outlook group.

TABLE 4.1 OUTLOOK GROUP FOLDERS

FOLDER	DESCRIPTION
Inbox	Includes messages you've sent and received by email and fax

FOLDER	DESCRIPTION
Calendar	Contains your appointments, events, scheduled meetings, and so on
Contacts	Lists names and addresses of the people with whom you communicate
Tasks	Includes any tasks you have on your to-do list
Journal	Contains all journal entries, such as phone logs, meeting notes, and so on
Notes	Lists notes you write yourself or others
Deleted Items	Includes any items you've deleted from other folders

THE MAIL GROUP FOLDERS

The Mail group folders provide a method of organizing your incoming and outgoing email messages. Table 4.2 describes each folder in the Mail group.

TABLE 4.2 MAIL GROUP FOLDERS

FOLDER	DESCRIPTION
Inbox	Contains all received messages
Sent Items	Stores all messages you've sent
Outbox	Contains messages to be sent
Deleted Items	Holds any deleted mail messages

I See Other Folders in My Groups You can add additional folders and folder icons very easily to Outlook. If you find folders other than the ones described here, folders have probably been added to your particular installation of Outlook.

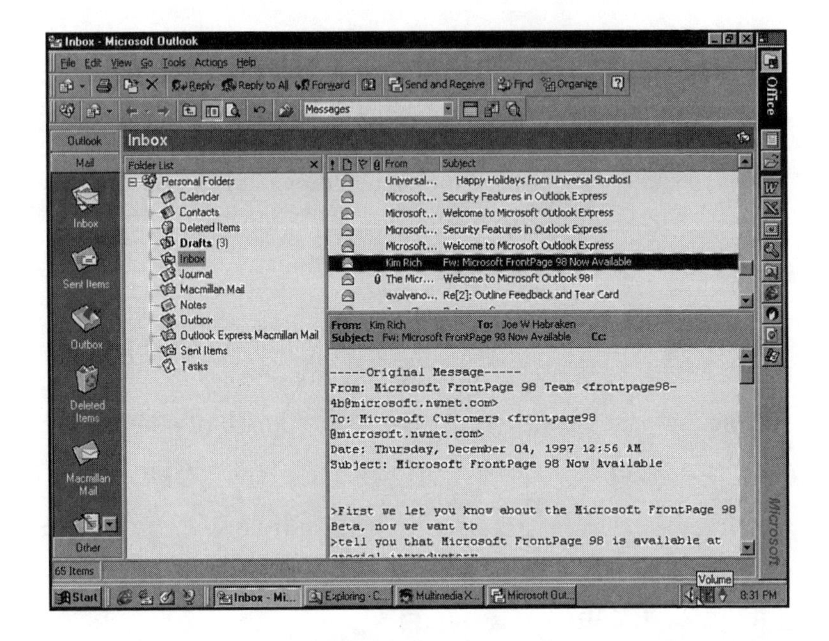

FIGURE 4.2 The Mail Group folder icons give you access to your email and fax messages that have been received, sent, are waiting to be sent, or have been deleted.

THE OTHER GROUP FOLDERS

The Other group contains folders that are on your computer but not within Outlook: My Computer, My Documents, and Favorites. You can access a document or information in any of those areas so that you can attach it to a message, add notes to it, or otherwise use it in Outlook.

For example, with My Computer, you can view the contents of both hard and floppy disks, CD-ROM drives, and so on (see Figure 4.3). Double-click a drive in the window to view its folders and files. Double-click a folder to view its contents as well. Then you can attach files to messages or otherwise use the files on your hard drive with the Outlook features.

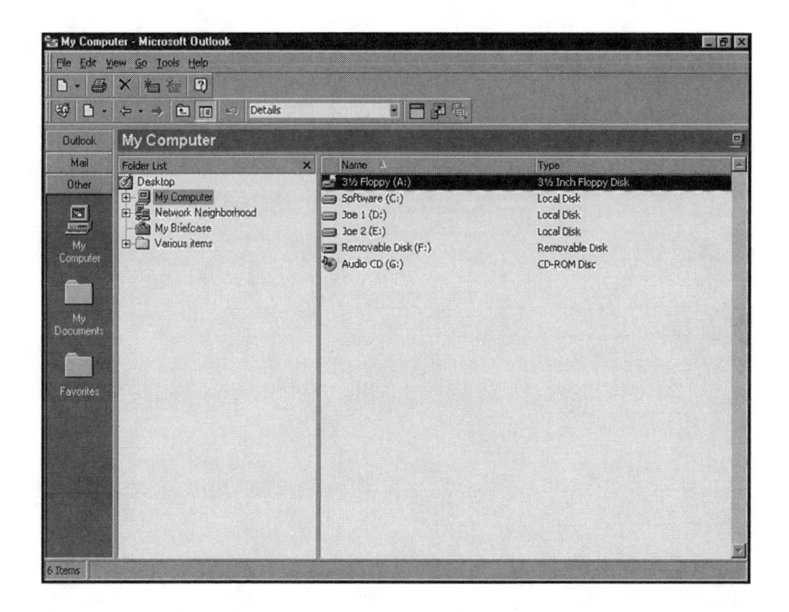

FIGURE 4.3 View your entire system through the My Computer folder in Outlook.

Moving On Up Use the Up One Level toolbar button to return to a folder or drive after you've double-clicked to expand it and view its contents.

USING THE FOLDER LIST

Outlook provides another method of viewing the folders within Outlook and your system: the Folder List. The Folder List displays the folders within any of the three groups (Outlook, Mail, or Other). From the list, you can select the folder you want to view.

To use the Folder List, first select the group you want to view from the Outlook Bar. Then click the Folder list button to display the list (see Figure 4.4).

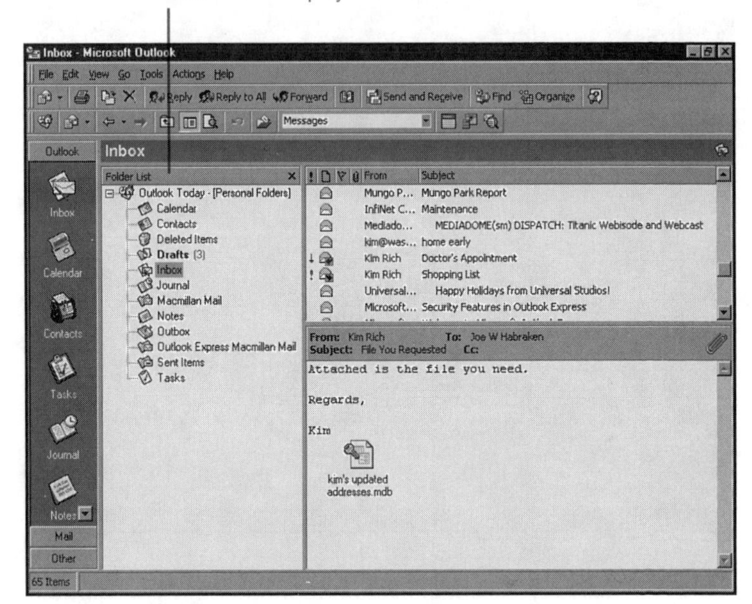

FIGURE 4.4 The Folder List shows all folders in the group you selected.

Choose any folder from the list, and the Information Viewer changes to reflect your selection. If you display another folder in the Information screen, double-click the folder to display its contents.

A View of the Folder List You can also open the folder list by using the View menu.

CHANGING VIEWS

In Outlook, views give you different ways to look at the same information in a folder. Each view presents the information in a different format and organizational structure so you can get the most from the program.

The easiest way to select the different views provided for each of your Outlook folders is a View box that is present on the Advanced toolbar for each folder type (Inbox, Calendar, Contacts, and so on). To open the Advanced toolbar for any Outlook folder, follow these steps:

1. Point to the Standard toolbar for an Outlook folder (such as the Inbox) and click the right mouse button.
2. A shortcut menu will appear, as shown in Figure 4.5. Click Advanced. The Advanced toolbar will appear.
3. You may want to close the Standard toolbar after you've opened the Advanced toolbar. Right-click either toolbar and then click Standard to remove the checkmark. The Standard toolbar will close.

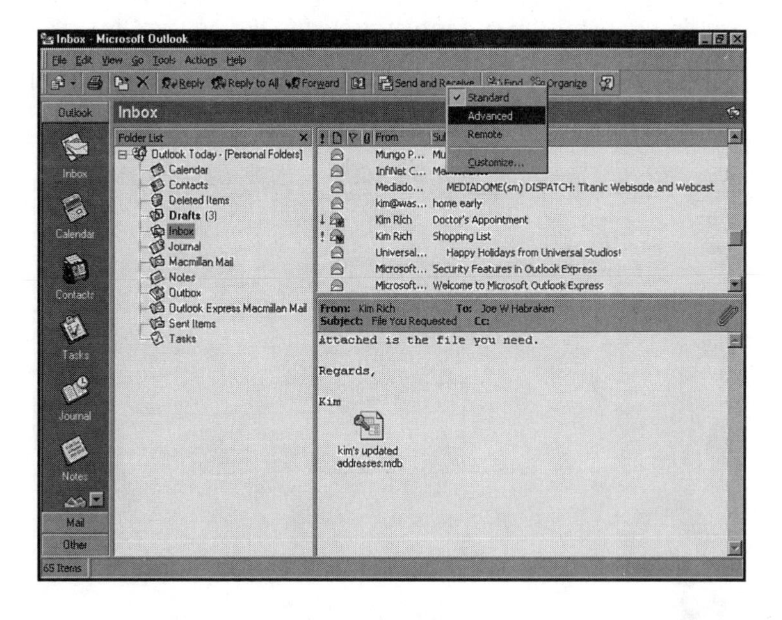

FIGURE 4.5 Right-click the Standard toolbar to open the Outlook Advanced toolbar for any folder.

You Only Have to Open the Advanced Toolbar Once After you've opened the Advanced toolbar for a folder, such as the Calendar or Inbox, it will be available for all the other Outlook folders.

Each folder—Inbox, Calendar, Contacts, and so on—will have a different set of buttons on the Standard and Advanced toolbars. This is because the commands and features that you access on a toolbar will be particular to the folder that you currently have selected.

After you have the Advanced toolbar open, you can change the current view by clicking the Current View drop-down box, as shown in Figure 4.6. Each Current View box contains views that are appropriate for the currently selected folder on the Outlook bar.

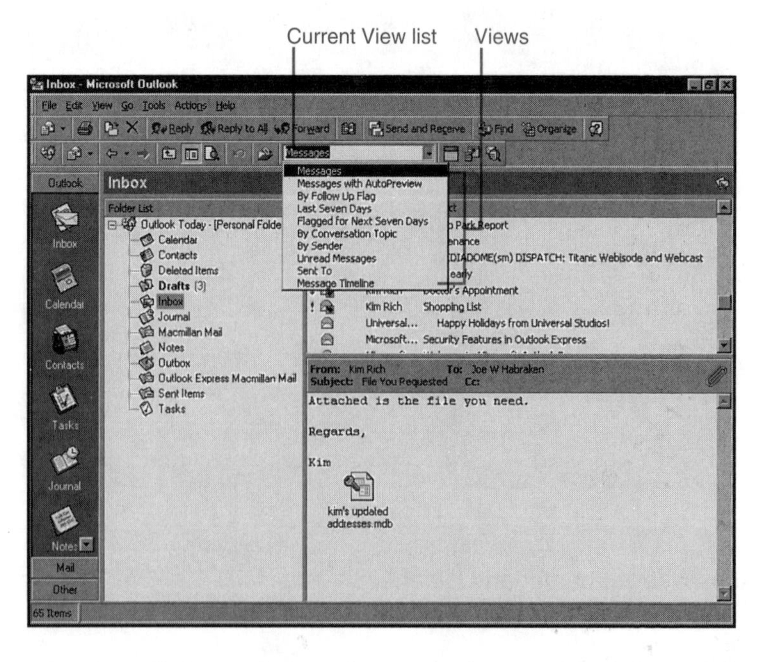

FIGURE 4.6 Select a view to change the format of the information.

As you can see in Figure 4.6, you can change your view of the Inbox, so that you can see all messages (Messages), messages and their first three lines of text (Messages with AutoPreview), messages that have been tagged with a follow-up flag (By Follow Up Flag), messages from the last seven days (Last Seven Days), messages tagged with a flag for the next seven days (Flagged for Next Seven Days), messages organized by topic (By Conversation Topic), messages organized by sender (By Sender), unread messages only (Unread Messages), messages by recipient (Sent To), and messages arranged in a timeline (Message Timeline).

Similarly, the Calendar folder—which is arranged in the Day/Week/Month view type by default—enables you to view your appointments and events by active appointments, Day/Week/Month with AutoPreview, events, recurring appointments, and several other view types.

You can also change the view type for any of your folders by selecting the Edit menu and then pointing at Current View. The View list appears as a submenu of Edit.

As you work your way through this book, you'll see examples of each view type. When you change folders in Outlook, take a quick look at the available views in the Current View drop-down list.

Creating Custom Views

You can also create custom views of the information in your Outlook folders. To create a custom view for one of your Outlook folders, follow these steps:

1. Click the Edit menu, and then point at Current View. Select Define Views. A Define Views dialog box for the currently selected folder will open.
2. Click the New button in the Define Views box. The Create a New View dialog box will appear as shown in Figure 4.7.

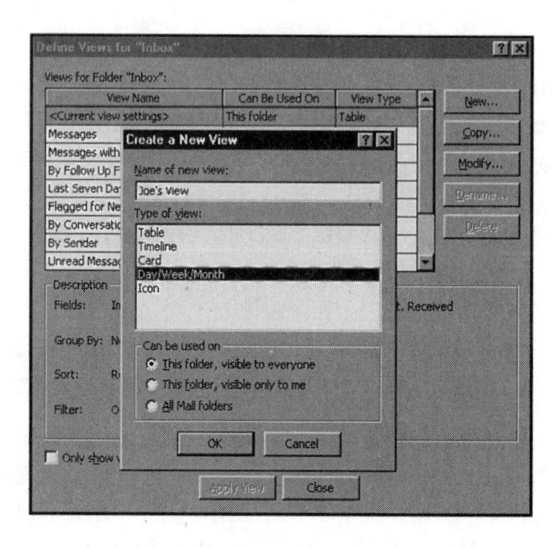

FIGURE 4.7 You can create custom views for your Outlook folders.

3. Enter a name for your new view and select a view type from the list in the Type of View box.

   The different view types that you can select for a custom view are described as follows:

   - **Table view** Presents items in a grid of sorts—in rows and columns. Use this view type to view mail messages, tasks, and details about any item.
   - **Timeline view** Displays items as icons arranged in chronological order from left to right on a time scale. Use this to view journal entries and other items in this type of view.
   - **Day/week/month view** Displays items in a calendar view in blocks of time. Use this type for meetings and scheduled tasks.
   - **Card view** Presents items like cards in a card file. Use this to view contacts.
   - **Icon view** Provides graphic icons to represent tasks, notes, calendars, and so on.

4. After you've selected the type of view you want to create, click the OK button. A View Settings dialog box appears. In this box you determine which fields you want to have in the view and the fonts and other view settings you want to use.

5. After you've selected the fields and view settings, click Apply View. The items in the current folder will appear in the new view.

Fields A specific type of information that you want to appear in your custom view. For a custom Inbox view using the Timeline view type, the fields would include Received (when the message was received), Created (when the message was created), and Sent (when the message was sent).

Your new view will appear on the Current View list on the Advanced toolbar. You can select it by clicking the list's drop-down arrow and then clicking the custom view's name.

Should I Design My Own Views? Designing your own views can prove to be complicated. Outlook provides several views for each of the folders on the Outlook Bar. You may want to explore all these possibilities before you begin to create your own views.

USING OUTLOOK TODAY

A great way to get a snapshot view of your day is Outlook Today. This feature provides you with a window that lists all your messages, appointments, and tasks associated with the current day.

To open the Outlook Today window, click the Go menu, then select Outlook Today. Icons for your Calendar, Messages, and Tasks appear in the Outlook Today window as shown in Figure 4.8. Items for the current day are listed below the icons.

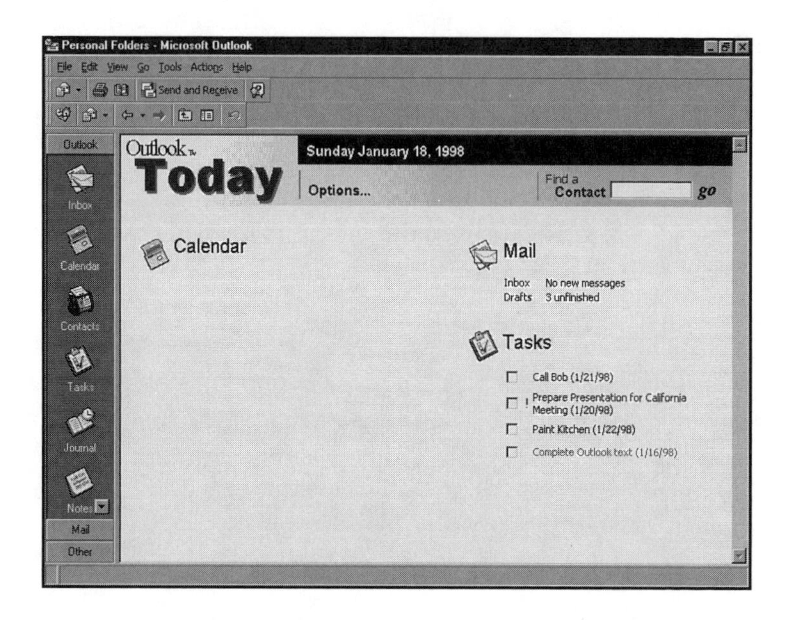

FIGURE 4.8 Outlook Today provides you with a list of all the items associated with the current day.

You can click any of the listed items (a particular appointment or task) to open the appropriate folder and view the details associated with the items. You can even update the items.

The Outlook Today window also provides you with a Find a Contact box that you can use to find people in your Contacts folder. Type a name in the Person text box and then click the Go button. A Contact window appears for the person. You can edit the person's information or close the Contact box by clicking the Close button.

After you have viewed the items in the Outlook Today window, you can return to any of your folders by clicking their icon on the Outlook Bar. Outlook Today is an excellent way to get a handle on what your day has in store for you.

In this lesson, you learned to use the Outlook Bar, change and create views in Outlook, use the Folder list, and take advantage of the Outlook Today feature. In the next lesson, you learn to get help in Outlook.

GETTING HELP

In this lesson, you learn to use the Office Assistant, to search for help on specific topics, and to use other Help features.

USING THE OFFICE ASSISTANT

You've probably noticed the Office Assistant: He's the paper clip (or other special character) in his own window. You can use the Office Assistant to help you with procedures, explanations, and tasks you perform in Outlook.

To use the Office Assistant, do one of the following:

- Click the Assistant window.
- Choose Help, Microsoft Outlook Help.
- Press F1.

The Assistant displays the help box shown in Figure 5.1. Office Assistant's help is context-sensitive; thus, depending on where you are in the program, the Assistant tries to offer help on related topics. If you need help on one of the suggested topics, click one of the blue option buttons.

Context-Sensitive A help feature that senses where you are in the program—in the Inbox, using the Calendar, or creating a message, for example—and offers help on topics that are related to your current task.

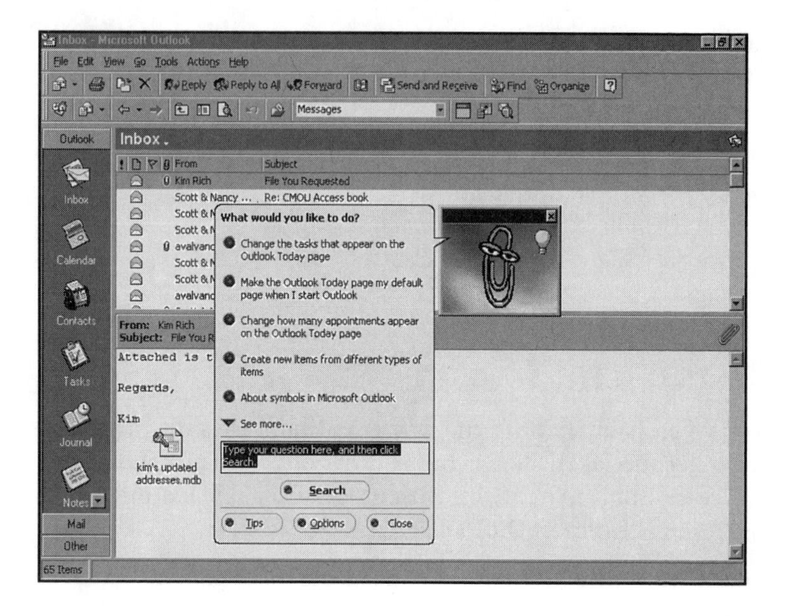

FIGURE 5.1 Use the Office Assistant to get context-sensitive help in Outlook.

If you need help on another topic, you can enter a question in the text box and click Search. You might, for example, enter "How do I print?" (or "How do I save a file?" or any other question containing key words related to topics for which you need help). When the Office Assistant box appears, it contains options related to your question.

To close the Office Assistant, click the Close button or click outside the help box.

Tricks of the Trade Click the light bulb in the Assistant's window to see a tip; click the Next button to view another tip; click the Close button to close the tip box.

You can right-click the Office Assistant and choose Hide Assistant from the shortcut menu. You can view tips from the shortcut menu. You also can choose options for the Assistant, including the type of tips displayed, the type of help you get with the Assistant, and so on.

Choosing a Different Assistant Outlook 98 and Microsoft Office come with several different Office Assistants. To choose a new assistant, right-click the current assistant and select Choose Assistant from the shortcut menu. An Office Assistant Gallery box will appear. Use the Next or Back buttons to choose a new assistant, and then click OK (you may have to insert your Office CD into your CD-ROM drive to select a new assistant).

USING THE HELP CONTENTS FEATURE

Use the Help Contents to view Outlook's Help Topics. The Help Topics function is a sort of onscreen user manual, providing a series of "books" with "chapters" you can read. You can find out how to print, use the calendar, format text, share information, and more.

To use the Contents feature, follow these steps:

1. Choose Help, Contents and Index. The Help Topics window appears (see Figure 5.2).
2. Double-click any book icon topic in the list, or click the topic and click the Open button. A more detailed list of topics appears from which you can choose the document you want to view, or a help window will open.
3. Double-click any document topic (the icon is a page with a question mark on it), and a new Help window appears with the procedure or explanation of the topic you selected. Many of the Help windows contain buttons that further explain an action that you want to perform. Click the button for more help. Figure 5.3 shows the Help window that results from choosing the Printing book icon, the Print page icon, and then the Print an Item button.

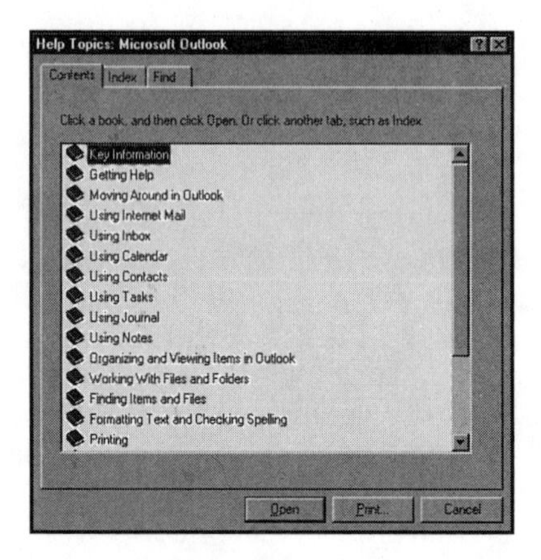

FIGURE 5.2 Find general information about tasks and procedures in the Contents section of Help.

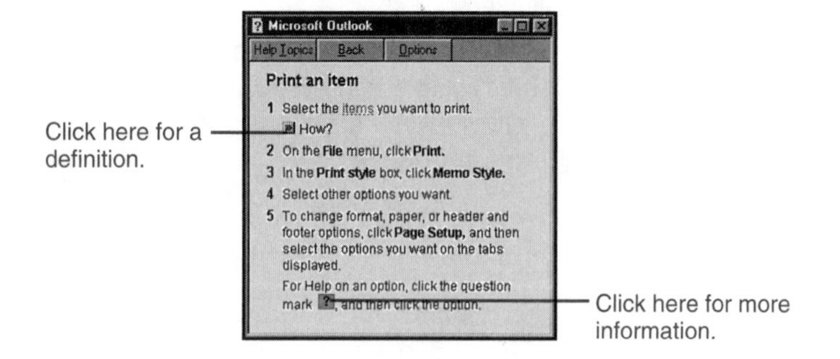

FIGURE 5.3 Let Help guide you through various processes in Outlook.

4. (Optional) To view the definition of any underlined word in a Help window, click the underlined word. Click the word a second time to close the definition box.

Help While You Work By default, the Help window stays on top of your work so you can refer to it as you follow the steps. If you'd prefer that the Help window not stay on top, open the Options menu, choose Keep Help on Top, and then select Not on Top.

5. (Optional) To find out more information, choose any of the gray buttons displayed in the Help text (refer to Figure 5.3).
6. When you're finished with Help, you can do any of the following:

   Print the topic by choosing Options, Print Topic.

   Click the Back button to view the previous Help window.

   Click the Help Topics button to go back to the Help Topics window.

   Click the Close (X) button to close Help.

SEARCHING WITH THE INDEX

Using the Help index, you can view or search through an alphabetical list of tasks and topics. *Topics* include Outlook features (usually in the form of nouns) such as Bulleted lists, Modem, or OLE. *Tasks* are actions you can perform in Outlook (in the form of verbs) such as Copying, Inserting, or Linking.

After you find the general task or topic you want in the Help Index, you can select a more specific topic or any of the related topics listed below it (see Figure 5.4).

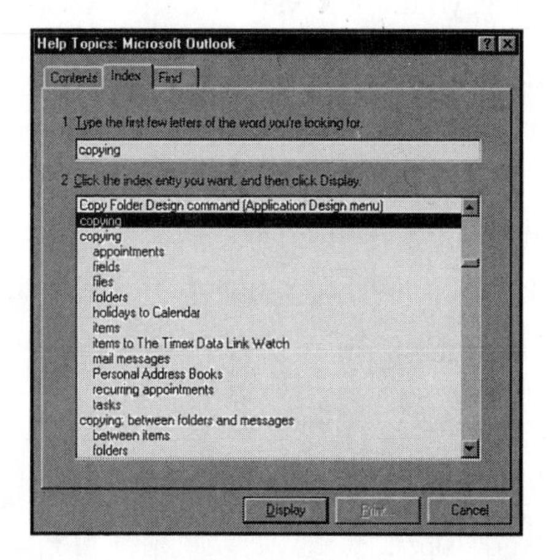

FIGURE 5.4 When you look up a task such as Copying, you can choose from several related topics (Files, Tasks, Messages, and so on).

To search for specific help using the Index, follow these steps:

1. In Outlook, choose Help, Contents and Index. The Help Topics window appears.
2. Click the Index tab.
3. In the text box, enter as many letters of the topic as necessary to narrow the search; as you type, the topic list jumps to the available listings that match what you type.
4. To view a specific topic, double-click it. Sometimes a dialog box appears listing more related topics; double-click the topic you want to view.
5. The Help window that appears is similar to the Help window that appears when you use the Contents help. You can print or close the Help window, or you can return to the Index Help window when you're done.

USING THE FIND TAB IN HELP

The Find tab lets you look for help in a different way. Find provides a method for narrowing the search related to a particular topic. For example, you might want information about printing. If you type the word "print" in the text box, a list of related words (such as printer, printing, printout, and so on) appears. You can let Outlook search for all of those topics, or you can narrow the search by typing more specific text such as "printout" or "prints."

To use the Find tab, follow these steps:

1. Choose Help, Contents and Index. The Help window appears.
2. Click the Find tab.

Setting Up Find The first time you use the Find tab, Outlook displays a dialog box asking if you want to set up the Find Help. Click the Next button, and a second dialog box appears. Click the Finish button, and Outlook sets up the Help database for you.

3. In the 1 Type the Word(s) You Want to Find text box, enter a word, topic, or phrase.

4. In the 2 Select Some Matching Words to Narrow Your Search list, click the topic you want to search for (see Figure 5.5). (To select multiple words listed next to each other, hold down the Shift key and click the first and last words. To select multiple items that are not adjacent, hold down the Ctrl key and click each one.)

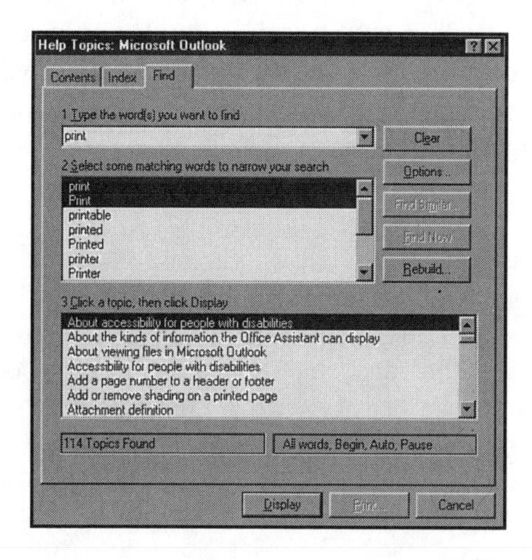

FIGURE 5.5 Find enables you to search for phrases as well as one-word topics.

5. Choose the topic you want from the 3 Click a Topic, then click Display list box. Click the Display button, and Outlook displays the Help window containing information related to the selected topic.

6. When you finish, click the Close (X) button to close the Help window or return to the Help Topics.

WHAT'S THIS?

In most of its dialog boxes, Outlook includes a handy tool called a What's This button. This is the question mark button that appears at the right end of the title bar next to the Close (X) button. You can click the What's This button and then click any item in the dialog box to see an explanation or definition of the selected element. Click again to hide the help box.

Another way to use this feature is to open the Help menu and choose the What's This command. When the mouse pointer changes to a pointer with a question mark, click anything in the Outlook window that you have a question about, and a Help box explaining the item appears.

Getting Help Without the Office Assistant If you find the Office Assistant to be more of a distraction than a help, you can get help without it. Right-click on the Assistant and then choose Options from the shortcut menu. Clear the Respond to F1 Key checkbox in the Office Assistant dialog box, then click OK. Click the Close button on the Assistant. Now the Assistant will no longer respond to your requests for help, and you will receive information using the "typical" Outlook Help system. You can also get additional help for Outlook and Office on the World Wide Web at **http://www.microsoft.com/office/**.

In this lesson, you learned to use the Office Assistant, to search for help on specific topics, and to use other Help features. In the next lesson, you learn to work with incoming mail.

WORKING WITH RECEIVED MAIL

LESSON 6

In this lesson, you learn to read your mail, save an attachment, answer mail, and close a message.

READING MAIL

When you log on to Outlook, your Inbox folder appears, and any new messages you've received are downloaded from your company's mail server. If you use Internet Mail, you will have to connect to your Internet Service Provider to download your mail using Outlook. Then any new mail will be placed in your Inbox (see Figure 6.1).

My Outlook Doesn't Open to the Inbox If Outlook opens to Outlook Today, click the Inbox folder on the Outlook Bar or click the Messages link in Outlook Today. Either of these alternatives will take you to your Inbox.

As you can see in Figure 6.1, the Inbox provides important information about each message. For example, one message has been labeled as high priority, one is low priority, and one message has an attachment. Messages that have already been replied to are marked with a curved reply arrow. You'll learn about priorities and attachments in Lesson 10, "Setting Mail Options." In addition, the status bar at the bottom of the Inbox window indicates how many items the Inbox folder contains and how many of those items are unread.

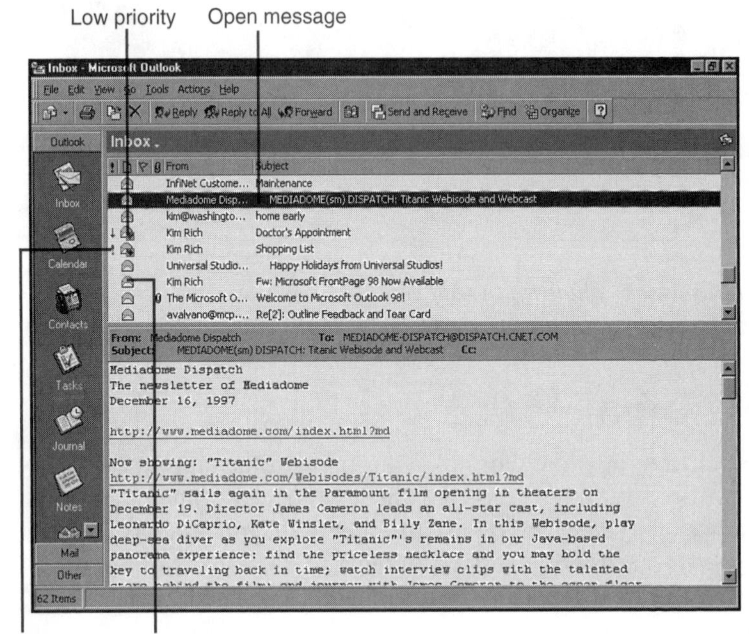

FIGURE 6.1 The Inbox provides information related to your received messages: the sender, subject, date received, and priority and attachment icons.

Welcome! The first time you log on, you may find an Outlook welcome message from Microsoft in your Inbox. After you read the message, you can delete it by selecting it and pressing the Delete key.

To read a message, you can click it, and its contents will appear in the Outlook Preview Pane. You can also open a message in its own window; double-click a mail message to open it. Figure 6.2 shows an open message.

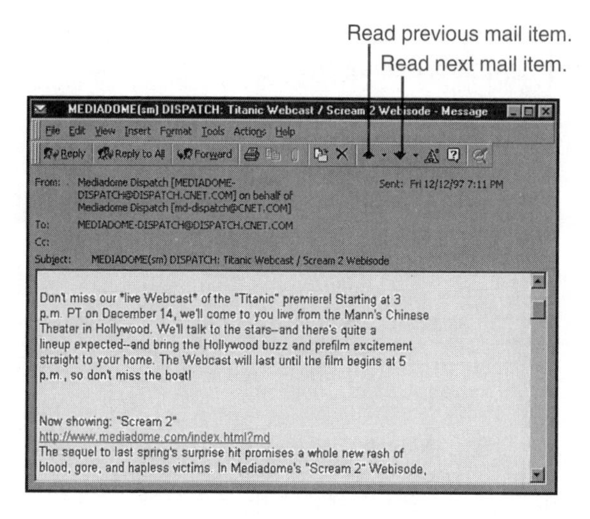

FIGURE 6.2 The Message window displays the message and some tools for handling this message or moving on to another.

To read the next or previous mail message in the Inbox, click the Previous Item or the Next Item button on the toolbar. Or you can open the View menu, choose Previous or Next, and choose Item.

> **Item** Outlook uses the word "item" to describe a mail message, an attached file, an appointment or meeting, a task, and so on. "Item" is a generic term in Outlook that describes the currently selected element.

You can mark messages as read or unread by choosing Edit, Mark as Read, or Mark as Unread. Outlook automatically marks messages as read when you open them. But you might want to mark messages yourself once in a while (as a reminder, for example). Additionally, you can mark all of the messages in the Inbox as read at one time by choosing Edit, Mark All as Read. You might want to mark mail messages as read so you don't read them again;

you might want to mark important mail as unread so you'll be sure to open it and read it again.

No Mail? If you don't see any new mail in your Inbox, click the Send and Receive button on the toolbar, or choose Tools, Check for New Mail, and Outlook will update your mail for you. Choose Tools, Check for New Mail On to specify a service other than the default. See Lesson 24, "Customizing Outlook," for more information.

SAVING AN ATTACHMENT

You will often receive messages that have files or other items attached. In the Inbox list of messages, an attachment is represented by a paper clip icon beside the message. You'll want to save any attachments sent to you so you can open, modify, print, or otherwise use the document. Messages can contain multiple attachments.

To save an attachment, follow these steps:

1. Open the message containing an attachment by double-clicking the message. The attachment appears as an icon in the message text (see Figure 6.3).

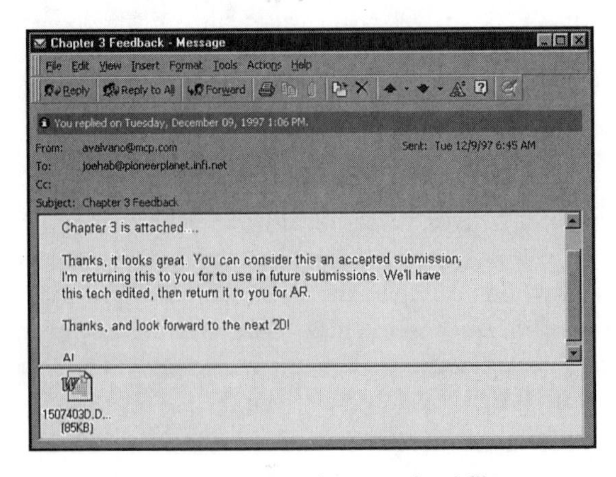

FIGURE 6.3 An icon represents the attached file.

2. (Optional) You can open the attachment from within the message by double-clicking the icon. The application in which the document was created—Word or Excel, for example—opens and displays the document in the window, ready for you to read. Close the application by choosing File, Exit.

3. In the message, select the attachment you want to save and choose File, Save Attachments. The Save Attachment dialog box appears (see Figure 6.4).

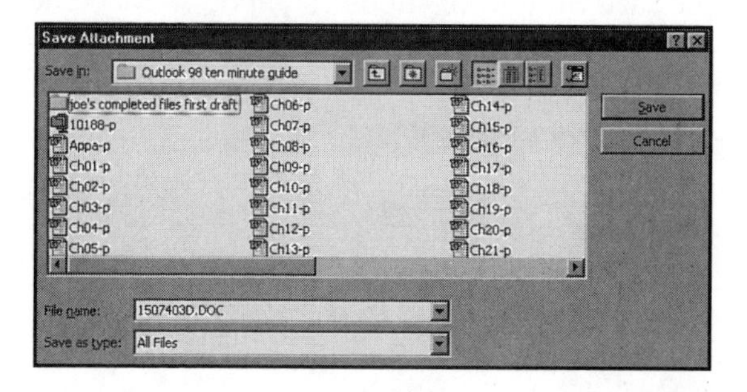

FIGURE 6.4 Save the attachment to a convenient folder.

4. Choose the folder in which you want to save the attachment, and click Save. You can change the name of the file, if you want. You can open the attachment at any time from the application in which it was created. The dialog box closes and returns to the Message window.

Use the Right Mouse Button You can also quickly save an attachment by right-clicking the attachment icon. On the shortcut menu that appears, click **Save As**, and then save the attachment to an appropriate folder.

ANSWERING MAIL

You might want to reply to a message after you read it. The Message window enables you to answer a message immediately, or at a later time if you prefer. To reply to any given message, follow these steps:

1. Select the message in the Inbox window and then click the Reply button on the Inbox toolbar.

   If the message is open, you can click the Reply button in the message window or choose Compose, Reply. The Reply Message window appears, with the original message in the message text area and the sender of the message already filled in for you (see Figure 6.5).

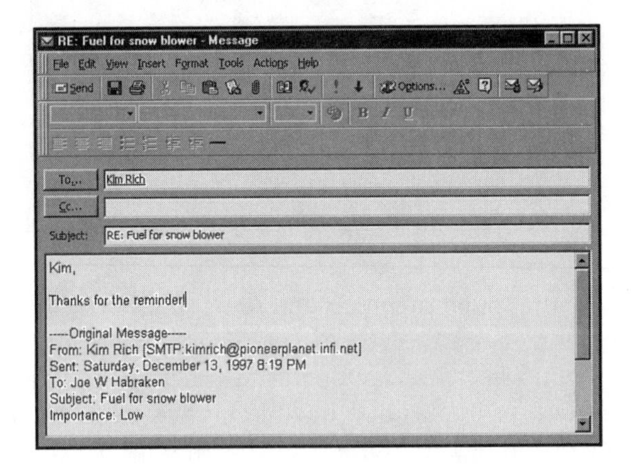

FIGURE 6.5 You can reply to a message quickly and easily.

Reply to All If you receive a message that has also been sent to others—as either a message or a "carbon copy" (Cc)—you can click the Reply to All button to send your reply to each person who received the message.

2. The insertion point is in the message text area, ready for you to enter your reply. Enter the text.

3. When you finish your reply, click the Send button or choose File, Send. Outlook sends the message.

If you are using Outlook as your Internet mail program, clicking the Send button only places the reply message in your Outlook Outbox. You must click the Send and Receive button on the Outlook toolbar to empty the Outbox and send your messages on to their respective recipients. You can also configure Outlook to send messages immediately. See Lesson 24 for information on customizing Outlook.

Reminder The next time you open a message to which you've replied, you'll see a reminder at the top of the Message tab that tells you the date and time you sent your reply. And don't forget that the purple arrow next to a message in the Inbox window shows that the message has been replied to.

PRINTING MAIL

You can print mail messages whether they're open or not. To print an unopened message, select the message in the message list of the Inbox or other folder and choose File, Print. If the message is already open, you can follow these steps:

1. Open the message in Outlook.
2. Use one of the following methods to tell Outlook to print:

- Click the Print button on the toolbar to print using defaults.
- Choose the File, Print command to view the Print dialog box.
- Press Ctrl+P.

3. In the Print dialog box, click OK to print one copy of the entire message using the printer's default settings.

More Print Info See Lesson 19, "Printing in Outlook," for detailed information about configuring pages, setting up the printer, and so on.

CLOSING A MESSAGE

When you finish a message, you can close it in any of the following ways:

- Choose File, Close.
- Click the Control-menu button and click Close.
- Press Alt+F4.
- Click the Close (X) button in the title bar of the Message window.

In this lesson, you learned to read your mail, save an attachment, answer mail, and close a message. In the next lesson, you learn to manage your mail messages.

LESSON 7

MANAGING MAIL

In this lesson, you learn to delete and undelete messages, forward messages, and organize messages by saving them to folders. You also work with the Outlook Rules Wizard and the Organize tool, which provide a way to automate certain mail management tasks.

DELETING MAIL

You may want to store some important messages, but you'll definitely want to delete much of the mail you receive after you've read it. After you've answered a question or responded to a request, you probably won't need a reminder of that transaction. You can easily delete messages in Outlook when you're finished with them.

To delete a mail message that is open, do one of the following:

- Choose File, Delete.
- Press Ctrl+D.
-  Click the Delete button on the toolbar.

If you have modified the message in any way, a confirmation message appears from the Office Assistant or as a message dialog box. Otherwise, the message is deleted without warning.

If you're in the Inbox and you want to delete one or more messages from the message list, select the single message to delete (or hold down the Ctrl key and click each message). Then do one of the following:

- Press the Delete key.
-  Click the Delete button on the toolbar.

UNDELETING ITEMS

If you change your mind and want to get back items you've deleted, you can usually retrieve them from the Deleted Items folder. By default, when you delete an item, it doesn't disappear from your system; it merely moves to the Deleted Items folder. Items stay in the Deleted Items folder until you delete them from that folder—at which point they are unrecoverable. To retrieve a deleted item from the Deleted Items folder, follow these steps:

1. Click the Deleted Items icon in the Outlook Bar to open the folder.
2. Select the items you want to retrieve, and drag them to the folder containing the same type of items on the Outlook Bar. Alternatively, you can choose Edit, Move to Folder and choose the folder to which you want to move the selected items.

EMPTYING THE DELETED ITEMS FOLDER

If you're really sure you want to delete the items in the Deleted Items folder, you can erase them from your system. To delete items in the Deleted Items folder, follow these steps:

1. In the Outlook Bar, choose the Mail group and then select the Deleted Items folder. All deleted items in that folder appear in the message list, as shown in Figure 7.1.
2. To permanently delete an item, select it in the Deleted Items folder and click the Delete button or choose Edit, Delete.
3. Outlook displays a confirmation dialog box asking if you're sure you want to permanently delete the message. Choose Yes to delete the selected item. You also can choose more than one item at a time by holding down the Shift or Ctrl key as you click each item.
4. To switch back to the Inbox or another folder, select the folder from either the Outlook Bar or the Folders List.

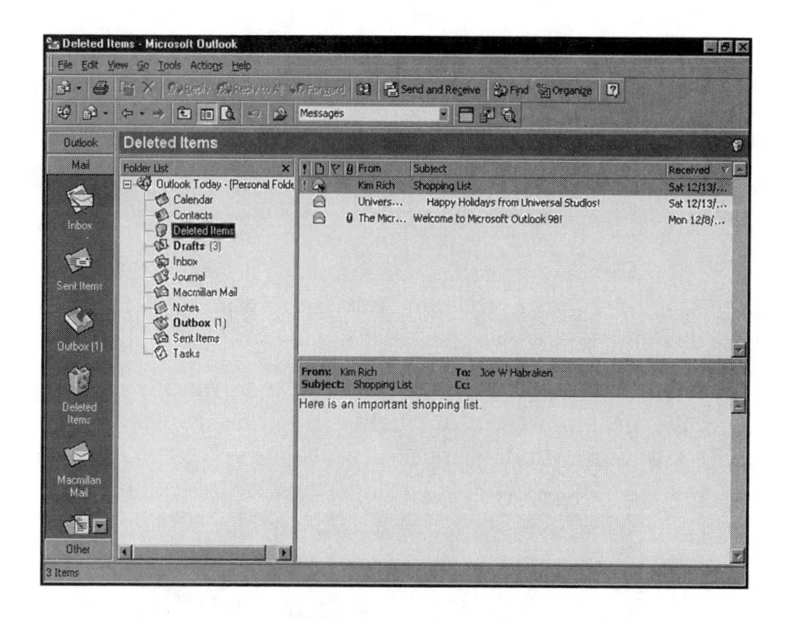

FIGURE 7.1 Deleted messages remain in the Deleted Items folder until you permanently delete them.

Automatic Permanent Delete You can set Outlook to permanently delete the contents of the Deleted Items folder every time you exit the program. To do so, choose Tools, Options, and click the General tab. In the General Settings area, select Empty the Deleted Items Folder Upon Exiting and click OK.

FORWARDING MAIL

Suppose you want to forward mail you receive from a coworker to another person who has an interest in the message. You can forward any message you receive, and you can even add comments to the message if you want.

Forward Mail When you forward mail, you send a message you received to another person on the network; you can add your own comments to the forwarded mail if you want.

You forward an open message or a message selected in the message list in the Inbox in the same way. To forward mail, follow these steps:

1. Select or open the message you want to forward. Then click the Forward button or choose Actions, Forward. The FW Message window appears (see Figure 7.2).

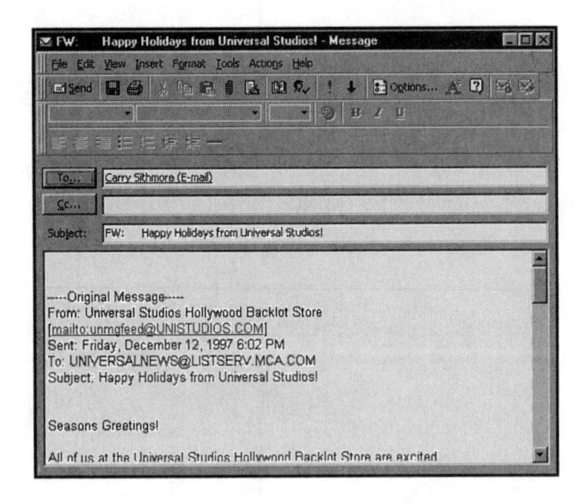

FIGURE 7.2 When you forward a message, the original message appears at the bottom of the message window.

2. In the To text box, enter the names of the people to whom you want to forward the mail. (If you want to choose a person's name from a list, click the To button to display the Select Names dialog box, and then select the person's name.) Lesson 8, "Using the Address Book," explains more about using the Address Book. If you enter

multiple names in the To box, separate the names with a semicolon and a space.

3. (Optional) In the Cc text box, enter the names of anyone to whom you want to forward *copies* of the message (or click the Cc button and choose the name from the list that appears).
4. In the message area of the window, enter any message you want to send with the forwarded text. The text you type will be a different color.

Attachments If the message that you forward contains attached files, the attachments will also be forwarded.

5. Click the Send button or choose File, Send.

SAVING MAIL TO A FOLDER

Although you'll delete some mail after you read and respond to it, you'll want to save other messages for future reference. You can save a message to any folder you want, but you should use a logical filing system to ensure that you can find each message again later. Outlook offers several methods for organizing your mail.

The easiest method of saving mail to a folder is to move it to one of Outlook's built-in Mail folders (as described in Lesson 3). You can use any of the folders to store your mail, or you can create new folders. Lesson 12, "Organizing Messages," describes how to create your own folders within Outlook.

To move messages to an existing folder, follow these steps:

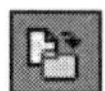

1. Select one message (by clicking it) or select multiple messages (by Ctrl+clicking). You can select an entire series of messages by clicking the first message and then Shift+clicking the last.

Making Backup Copies You can also copy a message to another folder as a backup. To do so, choose Edit, Copy to Folder.

2. Choose Edit, Move to Folder or click the Move to Folder button on the toolbar. The Move Items dialog box appears (see Figure 7.3).

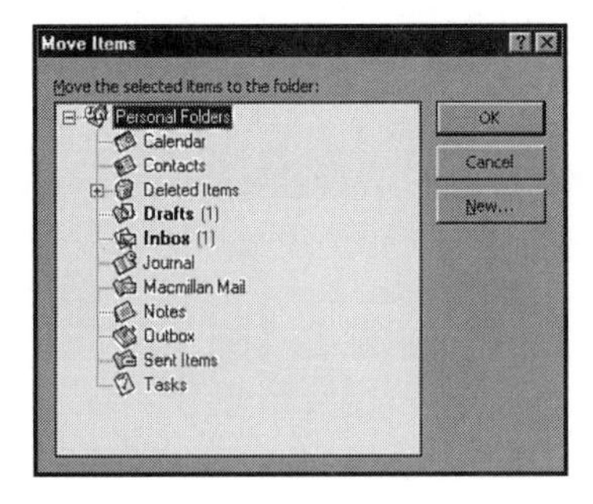

FIGURE 7.3 Choose the folder to which you want to move the selected message(s).

3. Select the folder to which you want to move the item and click OK. Outlook moves the item to the folder for you.

To view the message(s) you've moved, choose the folder from the Outlook Bar or the Folders List. Then click the item you want to view.

Attachments Move with Messages When you move messages to a folder other than the Inbox, any attachments to the message move to the new folder with the message. Attachments are really part of a message just as the text of the message is.

USING THE ORGANIZE TOOL

Outlook 98 provides an easy-to-use tool that can help you automatically move, delete, or color-code received and sent mail, called the Organize tool. The Organize tool can even help you deal with annoying junk email that you receive.

The Organize tool helps you to quickly create rules that govern what happens to messages that you receive from a certain person. For instance, you may want to move all the email that you receive from a particular client to a special folder automatically.

Rules A set of conditions (such as a particular email address, or message content) that you identify to move, delete, or manage incoming email messages.

Rules and Attachments The rules that you create to organize your messages can look at the sender, receiver, message subject, and message text. Attachments to a message are not governed by the rules that you create, and so the content of file attachments to a message do not govern how they are handled by the Organize tool or rules that you create.

To use the Organize tool to manage messages from a particular sender, follow these steps:

1. Select a message from the person in your Inbox.
2. Click the Tools menu, and then click Organize; or click the Organize button on the toolbar. The Organize window appears (see Figure 7.4).

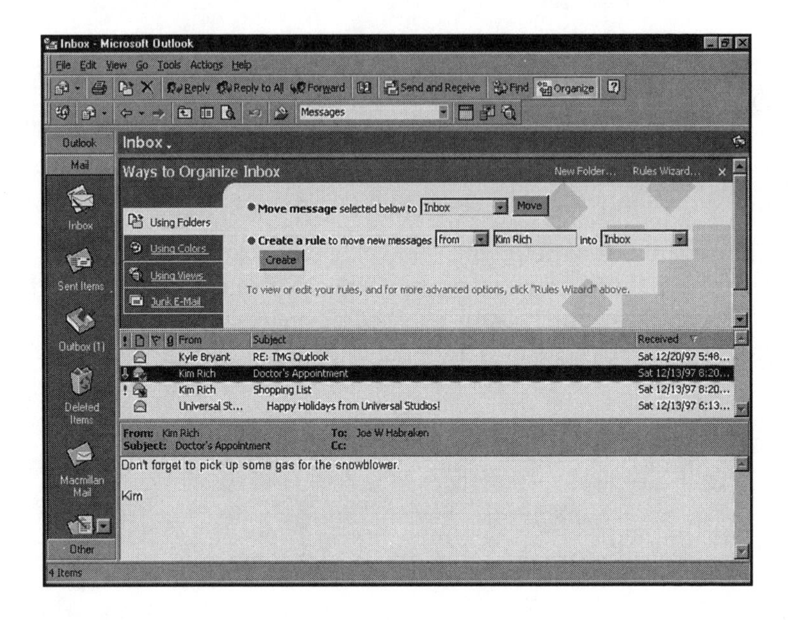

FIGURE 7.4 The Organize tool can help you manage messages using folders, colors, and views.

The Organize tool helps you manage and organize your messages using these methods:

- **Folders** This method is used to move or delete messages.
- **Colors** Color-codes the messages according to the rule you create.
- **Views** Uses the rule to categorize messages by their view (Flagged, By Sender, and so on).

A special category is also provided for dealing with junk email. To create a new rule related to the currently selected message in your Inbox, follow these steps:

1. Click Using folders. The email address of the person who sent you the selected email will appear in the From box.
2. In the Create a Rule to Move All Future E-mail box, click Received.

3. In the Other Folder box, click the name of the folder you want to move the messages to. If you want to move the message to a folder that is not listed on the drop-down list, click Other Folder.

4. When you have made your selections for each Organize text box, click Do It!.

You will get a message in the Organize window that **The rule was added successfully to the rules wizard**. If you chose Other Folder in the folder name box, the Select Folder box will appear; double-click the folder to which you want to move the incoming messages, and the rule will be completed.

The Organize tool also provides you with an automatic strategy for dealing with annoying junk mail. Click Junk E-mail in the Organize window. The Organize tool allows you to select the folders that corporate junk mail and adult junk are placed in when you receive them (see Figure 7.5). Outlook automatically identifies these types of mail messages as you receive them.

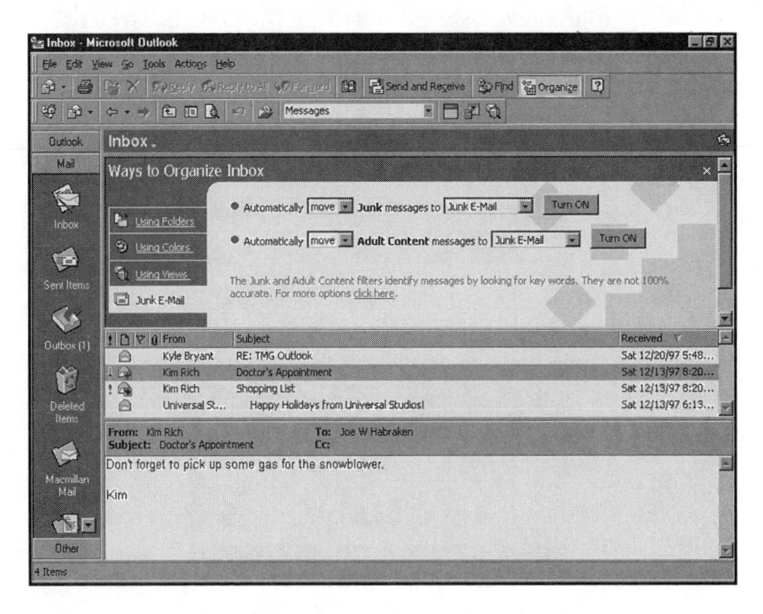

FIGURE 7.5 The Organize tool's Junk E-mail manager can help you deal with incoming junk mail.

You can also click the Junk E-Mail selection and add email addresses that you know to be the source of junk mail to a special junk email list. This can be very useful if certain junk mail is getting by the Organize tool's automatic junk mail filters for corporate and adult junk mail.

After you have completed your selections in the Organize window, click its Close button.

USING THE RULES WIZARD

If the Organize tool isn't able to do everything that you need it to do, you can create more advanced rules for managing messages using the Outlook Rules Wizard. The Wizard allows you to create rules using simple sentences that can do some pretty sophisticated things.

To open the Rules Wizard, follow these steps:

1. Click Tools, then Rules Wizard. The Rules Wizard dialog box appears (see Figure 7.6).

   All the rules previously created using the Organize tool will appear in the Rule Description box. You can copy, modify, rename, or delete a rule in this dialog box. You can also change a rule's priority by selecting a rule and then moving it up or down using the Move up or Move down buttons.

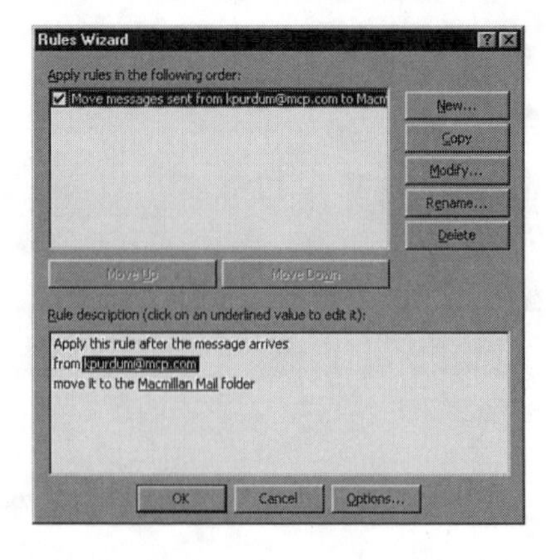

FIGURE 7.6 The Rules Wizard helps you create rules for managing mail messages.

2. To create a new rule, click the New button. The Rules Wizard walks you through the rule creation process. The first screen asks you to select the type of rule you want to create, such as Check Messages When They Arrive, or Notify Me When Important Messages Arrive (see Figure 7.7)
3. Select the type of rule you want to create, and then click Next.

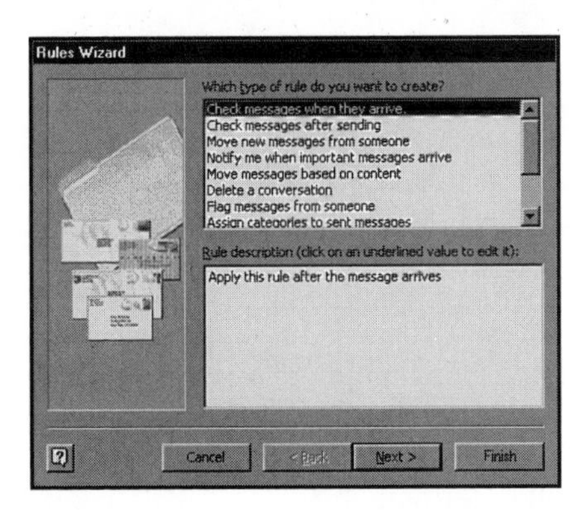

FIGURE 7.7 In the Rules Wizard, you select the type of rule you want to create.

4. The next screen asks you to select conditions that will be used by the new rule. These conditions range from messages sent directly to you, to specific words in the body of the message, to email addresses that you have placed on your junk email list. Use the check boxes provided to select the condition or conditions for your new rule. Click Next to continue.

Conditions That Require Input from You Some conditions such as "with specific words in the body," or "from people or distribution list" require that you provide a list of words or people for the condition to use. Conditions requiring additional information have an underlined selection for you to click.

5. The next screen asks you to decide what the rule should do to a message that meets the rules criteria. Several choices are provided, such as Move It to the Specified Folder, or Delete It (see Figure 7.8). Make your selections in the check boxes provided. Then click Next to continue.

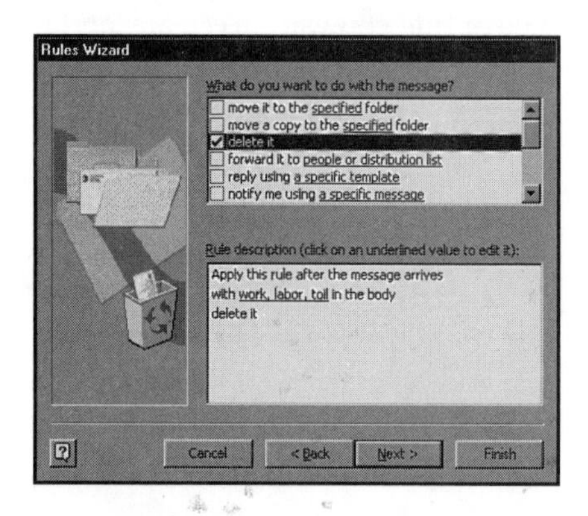

FIGURE 7.8 You determine the type of action you want Outlook to take when it finds a message that meets the rule's criteria.

6. The next screen provides you with the opportunity to add any exceptions to the rule. These exceptions can include Except If Sent Only to Me or Except Where My Name Is Not in the To or Cc Box. You add them by clicking the check box next to a particular exception. You can select multiple exceptions or choose to have no exceptions to the rules. Then click Next to continue.

7. The Rules Wizard's final screen asks you to type a name for your new rule. After you've done that, click Finish. The new rule will appear in the Rules Wizard dialog box. You can create more new rules or click OK to close the dialog box.

When you use the Rules Wizard for the first time, you may want to create a simple rule or two that handles messages that you do not consider extremely important. A poorly designed rule could delete important messages that you receive. A good rule of thumb is to use the Organize tool first and let it create simple rules, and if you need more advanced message management help, use the Rules Wizard.

In this lesson, you learned to forward messages, delete messages, and organize messages by saving them to folders. You also learned how to use the Organize tool and the Rules Wizard to help you manage your email messages. In the next lesson, you learn to work with address books.

Using the Address Book

In this lesson, you learn to use Outlook's address book with your email.

Using the Postoffice Address List

If you use Outlook as your email client on a corporate mail server, many of the messages you send will be to coworkers on that same network. The email addresses for these people will be determined by your network administrator. Outlook can also be set up to serve as your Internet email client.

Internet email Internet email is sent over the Internet by means of a modem or your corporate network. Internet email addresses usually take the form of *username@company.com.*

If you use corporate email, such as Microsoft Mail, to communicate with your coworkers, all of the email names within your organization usually appear on the Postoffice Address List created by your system's mail administrator. Whenever you want to send or forward an email, you can select the recipients from that list instead of typing in their names manually (or entering them in one of the other Outlook Address books or Contact lists). If you're using Windows NT on a network, you may or may not have access to the Postoffice Address List, depending on your permissions and rights. If you have a question, see your network administrator.

Post Office A directory, usually located on the network server, that contains a mailbox for each email user. When someone sends a message, that message is filed in the recipient's mailbox until the recipient receives the mail and copies, moves, or deletes it.

Postoffice Address List A list of everyone who has a mailbox in the post office; it's controlled by the mail administrator.

Mail Administrator The person who manages the email post office. (This person might also be the network administrator, but it doesn't necessarily have to be the same person.)

To use the Postoffice Address List, choose Tools, Address Book or click the Address Book button on the toolbar. The Address Book dialog box appears, as shown in Figure 8.1.

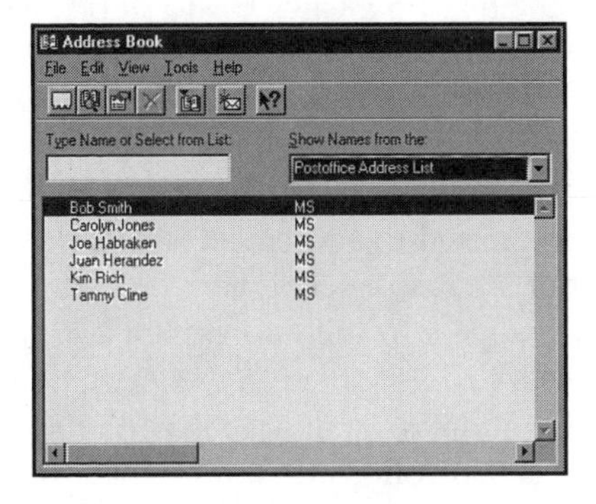

FIGURE 8.1 View the Postoffice Address List.

The following list outlines some of the ways in which you might use the Address List:

- To view more details about any entry in the Address Book dialog box (which contains the Postoffice Address List), double-click the person's name or click the Properties button on the toolbar. The person's Properties dialog box appears, with his or her name, address type, Postoffice name, and network type listed on the Address (1) tab. Click OK to close this dialog box and return to the Address Book dialog box.

- Click the Properties button on the toolbar and choose the Business tab in the person's Properties dialog box to view his or her phone number, office, or department, and any notes or comments that have been added to the description. Click OK to close this dialog box and return to the Address Book dialog box.
- To send a message to someone listed in the Address Book, select the name from the Address List and choose File, New Message. See Lesson 8 for more information.

- If you cannot find a particular name in the list, you can search for it. Choose Tools, Find or click the Find button, and then enter the name for which you're searching in the Find Name text box. Click OK to start the search.

If your corporation or organization uses Microsoft Exchange Server as its mail server, you can use Outlook as the email client, as you can for other email systems like Microsoft Mail or Internet mail. If you are connected to a Microsoft Exchange Server (the mail component of Microsoft NT Server), an additional list for mail addresses will appear in the Address Book drop-down list. You will have access to a list called *Global Address List*. This list, like the Post Office Address list described earlier for Microsoft Mail Postoffice groups, is controlled and maintained by your Network Administrator.

USING THE PERSONAL ADDRESS BOOK

The Personal Address Book contains the names and email addresses of people you contact frequently. You may want to include co-workers from your department, or even people from outside your office (whom you contact by using Internet addresses).

The Contacts Book You may notice Contacts in the list of address books; this book contains entries you create in your Contacts list. For more information about the Contacts list, see Lesson 15.

No Personal Address Book Is listed? If you do not see a Personal Address Book in the Address Book dialog box, you can easily add it to your resources. Close the address book and choose Tools, Services. In the Services tab of the dialog box, choose the Add button, and from the list, choose the Personal Address Book; then choose OK. Close the Services dialog box and open the address book again; you'll see the Personal Address Book in the list.

To add names to the Personal Address Book, follow these steps:

1. Choose Tools, Address Book, or click the Address Book button on the toolbar. The Address Book dialog box appears (refer to Figure 8.1).

2. To add name(s) from the Postoffice Address List, select the name(s) and click the Add to Personal Address Book button on the toolbar or choose File, Add to Personal Address Book. The name(s) remain on the Postoffice Address List, but Outlook copies them to your Personal Address Book as well. You can also add names from the Contacts list to the Personal Address Book in this manner.
3. To view your Personal Address Book, select the Show Names from the drop-down list and choose Personal Address Book. The list changes to display those names you've added to your personal address list, but the dialog box looks the same.

4. To add a completely new address to your Personal Address Book, click the New Entry button or choose File, New Entry. The New Entry dialog box appears (see Figure 8.2).

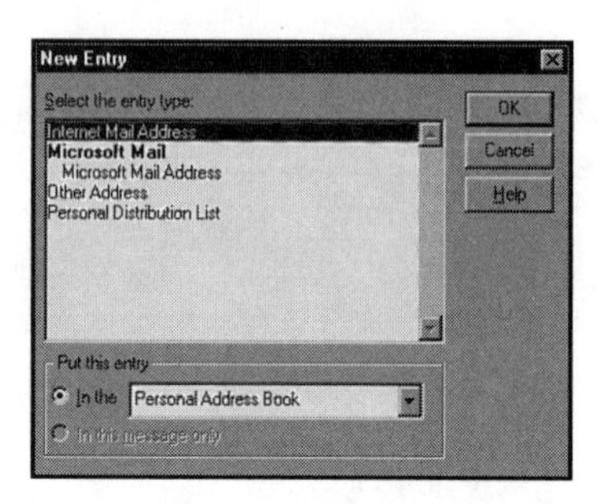

FIGURE 8.2 Choose a source for your new entry.

5. In the Select the Entry Type list, choose from the available options. The options you see will depend on the information systems installed on your network; for example, Microsoft Mail, Internet Mail, or some other service may be available. You can add an address entry that corresponds with one of the available information systems.

   Additionally, you can choose to add one of the following two items:

   Personal Distribution List Use this to create one address entry for a group of recipients. When you send mail to the list name, everyone on the list receives the message. You might use this option for grouping department heads, for example.

   Other Address Choose this option to add one new recipient at a time. You can enter a name, email address, and email type for each entry. In addition, you can enter business addresses and phone numbers, and you can add notes and comments to the entry. Use this entry for Internet addresses, for example.

6. When you're done working in your Personal Address Book, close the window by choosing File, Close. You return to the Outlook Inbox.

IMPORTING ADDRESS BOOKS AND CONTACT LISTS

If you are migrating from another personal information manager or email client and want to import your address book or contacts list, Outlook contains a number of different conversion filters for this purpose. Outlook even provides you with an Import/Export Wizard that walks you through the steps of importing address lists and address books from these other software packages.

To start the Outlook Import/Export Wizard, follow these steps:

1. Click File, then Import and Export. The Outlook Import and Export Wizard opens (see Figure 8.3).

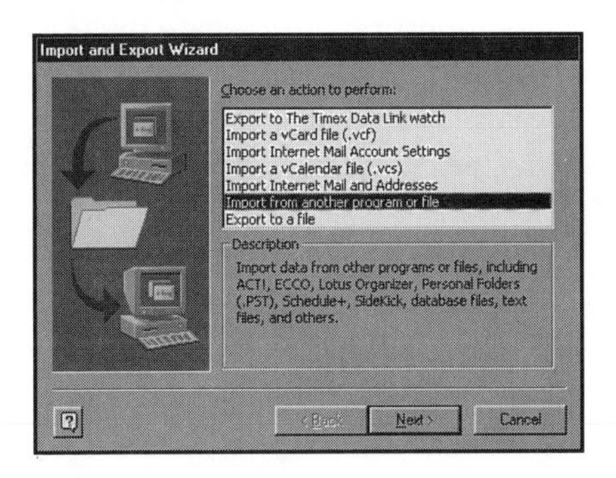

FIGURE 8.3 The Import and Export Wizard walks you through the process of importing your old address books.

2. On the first wizard screen, click Import from another program or file, then click Next. Conversion filters are available for popular personal information managers like Lotus Organizer and Sidekick. You can also import information from Microsoft Access and Microsoft Schedule Plus among others. Also any program that can save your former address book as a delimited file allows you to import the information into Outlook.

Delimited file Most database programs and personal information managers can save address books in a delimited format. This means that spaces or tabs are placed between the different fields of information. Saving an address book as a delimited file makes it possible to import the information into a number of different software packages that do not share the same file format as the software you are importing from.

3. Choose the program or file type that you want to use to import the address book, and then click Next.
4. The next wizard screen asks you to type in the name of the file you are importing or to locate the file on your computer using the Browse button. After you have selected the file, you can select one of the following option buttons:

   Replace duplicates with items imported

   Allow duplicates to be created

   Do not import duplicate items
5. After making your selections, click Next.
6. The next screen asks you to select the folder in which you want to place the new information. Because you are importing an Address Book, you will want to place the imported data into your Contacts folder. Click Next to continue.
7. The last screen asks you to match up the fields in the imported data with fields available in a typical Contacts form, such as Name, Address, Phone Number, Fax, and so on. Click the Map Custom Fields button to do this. The Map Custom Fields dialog box will appear.
8. Drag a field from the Import File box to the Outlook Contact box. Match fields that contain the same kind of data.

For example, if the import file contains a field for Phone, and you want this information to appear in the Contact Business phone field, drag the Phone field from the Import box and place it next to the Business Phone field in the Contacts box (see Figure 8.4).

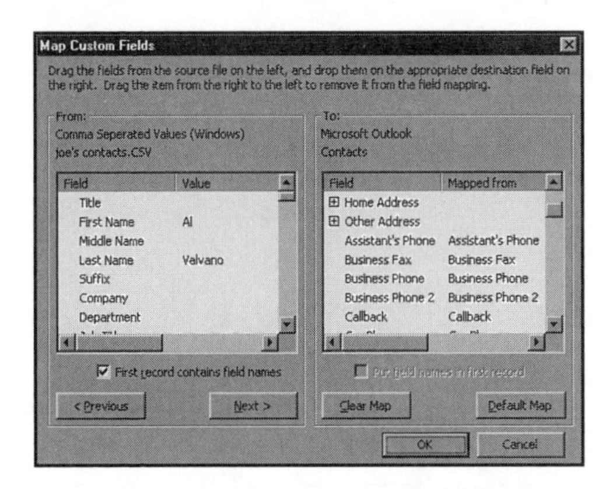

FIGURE 8.4 Match the fields in the import file with the fields in Contacts.

When you have completed matching the fields, click OK. You return to the final Wizard screen. Click Finish. The contact information from the import file will be placed in your Outlook Contact folder.

In this lesson, you learned to use the address book with your email and import address books from other software programs. In the next lesson, you learn to compose a message and format it.

LESSON 9

Creating Mail

In this lesson, you learn to compose a message, format text, check your spelling, and send mail. You also learn to use different email formats such as text-only and HTML mail.

Composing a Message

You can send a message to anyone for whom you have an address, whether his or her address is in your address book, your list of contacts, or scribbled on a Post-It note. In addition to sending a message to one or more recipients, you can send copies of a message to others on your various address lists.

Entering an Address in a Message

You can either use the address book to choose the names of recipients to whom you want to send new messages or have the email address automatically placed in the To: box when you forward messages or send a reply. Using the address book also makes sending carbon copies and blind carbon copies easy.

Blind Carbon Copy A blind carbon copy (Bcc) of a message is a copy that's sent to someone in secret; the other recipients have no way of knowing that you're sending the message to someone as a blind carbon copy.

To address a message, follow these steps:

1. Choose Compose, New Mail Message from the Outlook Inbox window, or click the New Message button on the toolbar. A new message window appears (see Figure 9.1).

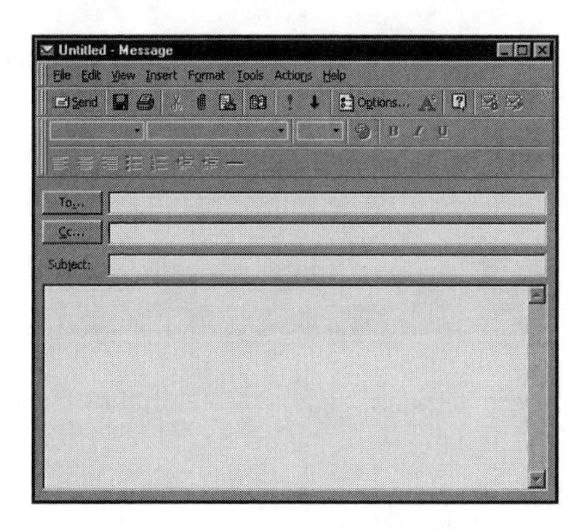

FIGURE 9.1 Compose a new message in the Untitled - Message window.

2. In the Message window, click the To button to display the Select Names dialog box.
3. Open the Show Names from the drop-down list box and choose the Postoffice Address List, Contacts List, Global Address List, or the Personal Address Book.
4. From the list that appears on the left, choose the name of the intended recipient and select the To button. Outlook copies the name to the Message Recipients list. (You can add multiple names if you want.)
5. (Optional) Select the names of anyone to whom you want to send a carbon copy, and click the Cc button to transfer those names to the Message Recipients list.
6. (Optional) Select the names of anyone to whom you want to send a blind carbon copy and click the Bcc button.

Figure 9.2 shows a distribution group listing as the To recipient of a message.

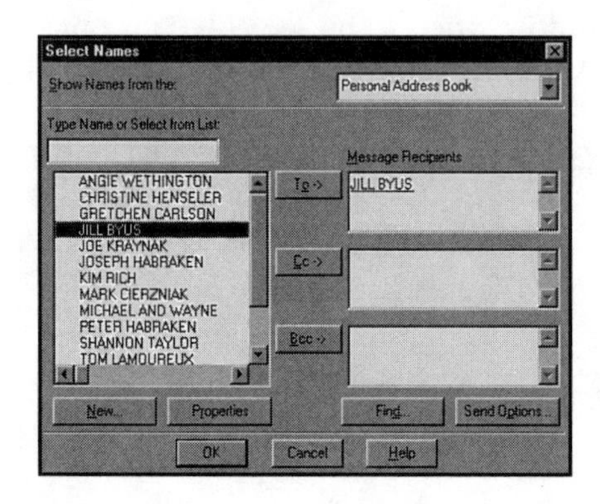

FIGURE 9.2 Address messages quickly with the Select Names dialog box.

7. Click OK to return to the Message window.

   You can also easily send email to any people whose addresses you keep in your Contacts folder. How to use and maintain the Contacts folder is covered in Lesson 15, "Creating a Contacts List."

8. Click in the text area, and then enter the text of the message. You do not have to press the Enter key at the end of a line; Outlook automatically wraps the text at the end of a line for you. You can use the Delete and Backspace keys to edit the text you enter.

9. When you finish typing the message, you can send the message to your OutBox (see "Sending Mail" later in this lesson), or you can check the spelling and formatting as described in the following sections.

No Address! If you try to send a message without entering an address, Outlook displays the Check Names dialog box, in which it asks you to create an address. You can search for the name among the existing addresses, or you can create a new address for the name in much the same way you would create a new entry in the Address Book (see Lesson 8).

FORMATTING TEXT

You can change the format of the text in your message to make it more attractive, to make it easier to read, or to add emphasis. Any formatting you do transfers to the recipient with the message if the recipient has Outlook or another email client that can work with Microsoft Exchange Rich Text or HTML messages. However, if the recipient doesn't have an email package that can handle these special message formats, formatting may not transfer. Many Internet email clients do not offer this capability. Most corporate email clients, such as Lotus Notes and Novell GroupWise, do allow the sending and receiving of messages in Rich Text Format. You should keep in mind that if you send a Rich Text or HTML message to a person who has an email client that cannot handle special formatting, they will receive the message in plain text.

Microsoft Exchange Rich Text A special email format developed by Microsoft for use with Microsoft mail systems. Outlook 98 can send and receive messages in the Exchange Rich Text format. This allows you to send and receive messages with special formatting such as bold, italic, fonts, and other special characters and graphics.

HTML Hypertext Markup Language is used to design Web pages for the World Wide Web. Outlook 98 can send messages in this format, providing you with a number of formatting options.

You format text in two ways. You can format the text after you type it by selecting it and then choosing a font, size, or other attribute; or you can select the font, size, or other attribute and then enter the text.

To format the text in your message, follow these steps:

1. If the Formatting toolbar is not showing, choose View, Toolbars, Formatting. Figure 9.3 shows a message with the Formatting toolbar displayed. Table 9.1 explains the buttons on this toolbar.

Formatting Toolbar Buttons Unavailable! If you've selected to send your messages as text-only, the Formatting toolbar buttons will be unavailable to you. Only messages sent in Microsoft Exchange Rich Text format or HTML format can be formatted. See the section in this lesson on "Sending HTML Mail" for more information. If you have installed Outlook for Internet email only, you will also find that when you select the Format command, only Plain Text and Rich Text (HTML) are available as choices.

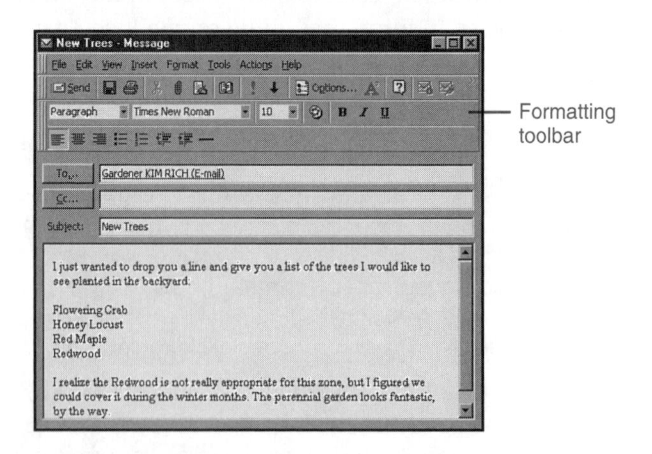

FIGURE 9.3 Use the Formatting toolbar to modify your message text.

Table 9.1 Formatting Toolbar Buttons.

Button	Name
 Paragraph	Style
 Times New Roman	Font
 10	Font Size
	Font Color
 B	Bold
 I	Italic
 U	Underline
	Align Left
	Center
	Align Right
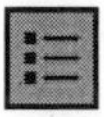	Bullets
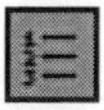	Numbering
	Decrease Indent
	Increase Indent
	Insert Horizontal Line

2. To apply a font to the selected or about-to-be-entered text, click the down arrow in the Font box on the Formatting toolbar. Scroll through the font list, if necessary, to view all fonts on the system, and click the font you want to apply to the text. You can also apply a style to selected text in the message. Click the Style drop-down arrow on the Formatting toolbar. The styles available range from a set of predefined heading styles to special styles such as Directory List and Menu List.

Quick Format You can also format text by choosing Format, Font and selecting a font, size, style, and so on from the Font dialog box. You also can assign bullets and alignment to text by choosing Format, Paragraph.

3. Assign a size by clicking the down arrow beside the Font Size drop-down list and choosing the size; alternatively, you can enter a size in the Font Size text box.
4. To choose a color, click the Color button and select a color from the palette box that appears.
5. Choose a type style to apply to text by clicking the Bold, Italic, and/or Underline buttons on the Formatting toolbar.
6. Choose an alignment by selecting the Align Left, Center, or Align Right button from the Formatting toolbar.
7. Add bullets to a list by clicking the Bullet button on the Formatting toolbar. If you prefer a numbered list, click the Numbering button.
8. Create text indents or remove indents in half-inch increments by clicking the Increase Indent or Decrease Indent buttons. (Each time you click the Indent button, the indent changes by half an inch.)

Using Undo If you assign formatting to your text and don't particularly like it, click Edit, Undo to remove the last formatting that you did.

SENDING HTML MESSAGES

Another alternative for sending messages with formatted text is the HTML format. HTML stands for Hypertext Markup Language and is the language used to design Web pages for the World Wide

Web. You can choose to send your email messages in this format by following these steps:

1. Click Tools, then Options. The Options dialog box will appear.
2. Click the Mail Format tab (see Figure 9.4).

Include hyperlinks If you send HTML or Rich Text Format messages, you can include hyperlinks. Hyperlinks are Web addresses and email addresses that can be accessed by clicking them in the message. Just type the Web address or email address, and the hyperlink will be created automatically.

3. To select the message format, click the Send in This Message Format drop-down box. Select HTML, Microsoft Exchange Rich Text, Plain Text, or Microsoft Word.
4. Click OK to close the dialog box.

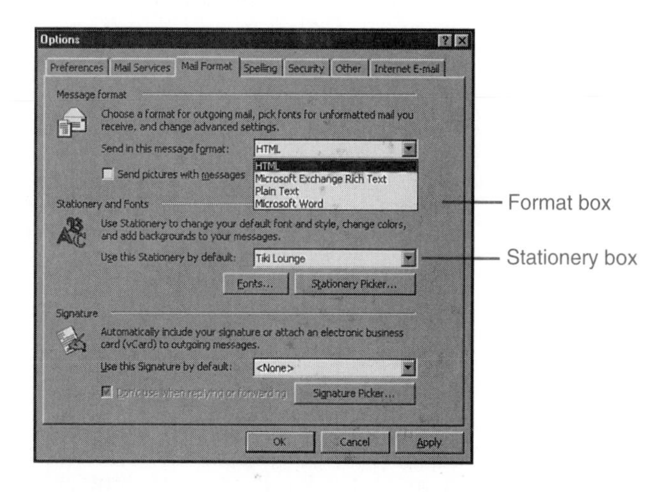

FIGURE 9.4 You can select to send your messages in HTML, Microsoft Exchange Rich Text, Plain Text, or Microsoft Word formats.

If you choose to use the HTML format in the Options box, you can also select special stationery to send your messages on. Click the Use This Stationery by Default drop-down box. Outlook provides a number of HTML stationery types. To see a preview of the stationery types listed, click Stationery Picker button.

Using the HTML format for your messages provides you with the greatest number of possibilities as far as formatting and graphics in email messages. Remember, however, that you can take advantage of the HTML format only if the receiver of your message is using Outlook or another email client that can read a message in HTML.

SENDING TEXT-ONLY MESSAGES

If you send most of your messages to recipients who do not use Outlook 98 or another email client that can take advantage of Rich Text or HTML-formatted messages, you may want to set your default message type to text only. This sends all your messages in plain text that can be read by all email clients.

To select Plain Text as your message format, follow these steps:

1. Click Tools, then Options. The Options dialog box appears.
2. Click the Mail Format tab.
3. Click the Send in This Message Format drop-down box, and select Plain Text.
4. Click OK to close the dialog box.

CHECKING SPELLING

To make a good impression and to maintain your professional image, you should check the spelling in your mail messages before you send them. Outlook includes a spelling checker you can use for that purpose. You'll notice your grammar is automatically checked, as well.

To check the spelling in a message, follow these steps:

1. In the open message, choose Tools, Spelling and Grammar, or press F7. If the spelling checker finds a word whose spelling it questions, it displays the Spelling dialog box (shown in Figure 9.5). If no words are misspelled, a dialog box appears saying the spelling and grammar check is complete; choose OK to close the dialog box.

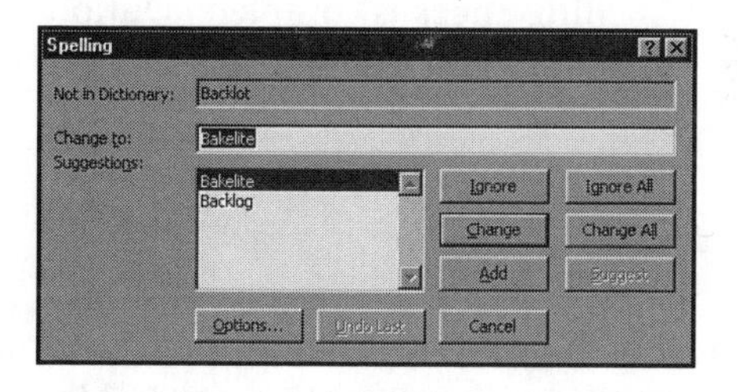

FIGURE 9.5 Check your spelling before sending a message.

2. You can do any of the following in response to the word Outlook questions in the Spelling dialog box:

   Not in Dictionary Enter the correct spelling in this text box.

   Suggestions Select the correct spelling in this text box, and it automatically appears in the Change To text box.

   Ignore Click this button to continue the spelling check without changing this occurrence of the selected word.

   Ignore All Click this button to continue the spelling check without changing any occurrence of the word in question throughout this message.

   Change Click this button to change this particular occurrence of the word in question to the spelling in the Change To text box.

   Change All Click this button to change the word in question to the spelling listed in the Change To text box every time the spelling checker finds the word in this message.

Add Click this button to add the current spelling of the word in question to the dictionary so that Outlook will not question future occurrences of this spelling.

Undo Click this button to reverse the last spelling change you made, thus returning the word to its original spelling.

Cancel Click this button to quit the spelling check.

3. When the spelling check is complete, Outlook displays a message box telling you it's done. Click OK to close the dialog box.

Set Your Spelling Options Click the Options button in the Spelling dialog box to set options that tell Outlook to do such things as ignore words with numbers, ignore original message text in forwarded messages or replies, always check spelling before sending, and so on.

SENDING MAIL

When you're ready to send your mail message, do one of the following:

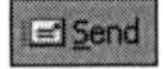

- Click the Send button.
- Choose File, Send.
- Press Ctrl+Enter.

AutoSignature Choose Tools, AutoSignature to have Outlook automatically add a message, quotation, or other text at the end of every message you send. Additionally, after you create an autosignature, you can quickly add it to any message by choosing Insert, AutoSignature.

Using Windows NT 4.0? You'll need to check your rights and permissions in relation to sending email within your network. Ask your system administrator for more information.

RECALLING A MESSAGE

If you configured Outlook for corporate email, you can recall messages that you send over your corporate network and over the Internet. You can only recall messages that have not been opened or moved to another folder. If you want to recall a message on your corporate network, the individual from whom you are recalling the message must be logged on.

To recall a sent message, follow these steps:

1. Click the Mail button on the Outlook Bar, and then select the Sent Items Folder.
2. Double-click to open the message that you want to recall.
3. In the Message window, click the Tools menu, then click Recall This Message. The Recall This Message dialog box will open.
4. To recall the message click the Delete Unread Copies of This Message option button, then click OK. A notice appears in the Message window (upper-left corner) letting you know that you are attempting to recall this message.
5. Click File, then Save to save the message with the recall option. Close the message.
6. You will eventually receive a notification in your Inbox (as new mail) notifying you whether or not the recall was successful.

In this lesson, you learned to compose a message, format text, check your spelling, and send mail. You also learned how to select different email formats such as HTML and Plain Text. You also learned how to recall a message. In the next lesson, you learn to set mail options and how to tell if the recipient has received your message.

SETTING MAIL OPTIONS

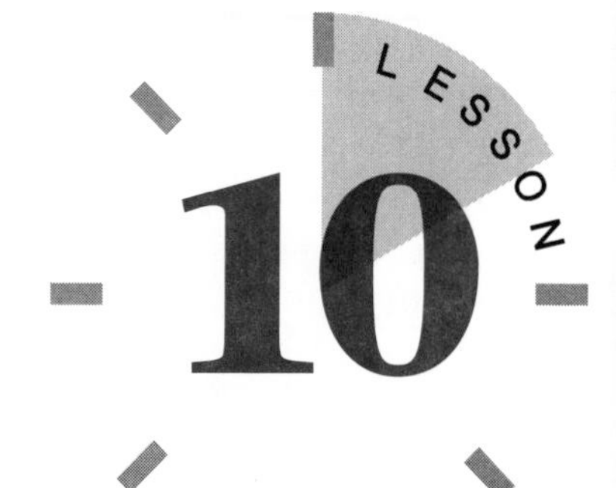

In this lesson, you learn to set options for messages and delivery, and for tracking messages.

CUSTOMIZING OPTIONS

Outlook provides options that enable you to mark any message with priority status so that the recipient knows you need a quick response, or with a sensitivity rating so your words cannot be changed by anyone after the message is sent. With other options, you can enable the recipients of your message to vote on an issue by including voting buttons in your message and having the replies sent to a specific location.

You also can set delivery options. For example, you can schedule the delivery of a message for a specified delivery time or date if you don't want to send it right now.

Recognizing Priority Flags Not all email packages will recognize the priority flags you place on messages you send. These priority flags work ideally in a network situation, where Outlook is the email client for all users. Results will vary for Internet email. Microsoft Outlook Express recognizes Outlook priority flags.

To set message options, open a new Untitled-Message window and click the Options button on the toolbar. As you can see in Figure 10.1, the Message Options dialog box is separated into four areas. The next four subsections discuss each group of options in detail.

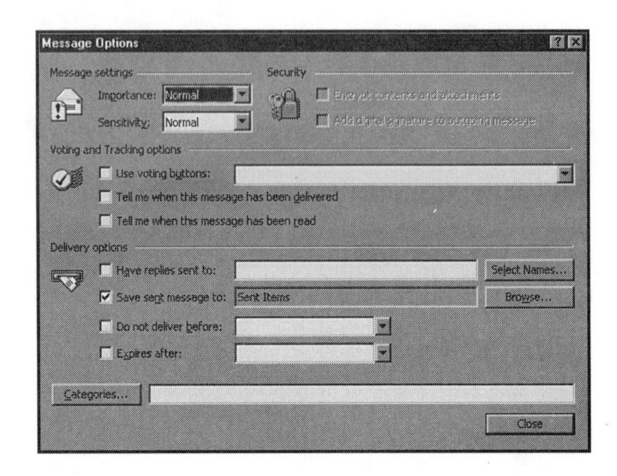

FIGURE 10.1 Use the Message Options settings to govern how your message is sent.

MESSAGE SETTINGS

In the Message Settings area, set any of the following options for your message:

- Click the Importance drop-down arrow and choose a priority level of Low, Normal, or High from the list. (Alternatively, you could click the Importance High or Importance Low button on the toolbar.) When importance isn't specified, the message is given Normal Importance.
- Click the Sensitivity drop-down arrow and choose one of the following options:

  Normal Use this option to indicate that the message contents are standard, or customary.

  Personal Use this option to suggest that the message contents are of a personal nature.

  Private Use this option to prevent the message from being edited (text changes, copy, paste, and so on) after you send it.

  Confidential Use this option to indicate that the message contents are restricted or private.

You Can Mark All Messages As Private You can mark all of your messages so that no one can tamper with your words by choosing Tools, Options and clicking the Sending tab. In the Set Sensitivity box, choose the level you want.

Outlook also supplies you with two security options. You can choose to encrypt the contents and attachments of a message: Click the Encrypt Contents and Attachments check box next to the Security icon. You can also add a digital signature to the message that verifies you are the sender: Click the Add Digital Signature to Outgoing Message check box.

Encryption Messages are coded so that they remain secure until the recipient opens them. The recipient is able to "decode" the message because he or she is identified by Digital ID.

Digital Signature A Digital ID that is electronically stamped on messages that you send.

Before you can use the encryption and digital signature features in Outlook 98, you must obtain a Digital ID. Digital IDs are issued by an independent certifying authority. Microsoft maintains a Web page—**http://www.microsoft.com/ie/ie40/oe/certpage.htm**—that lists a number of certifying authorities that provide Digital IDs. Each certifying authority provides a Web page that gives you the information that you need to obtain, download, and install your Digital ID.

VOTING AND TRACKING OPTIONS

The Voting and Tracking Options allow you to control special features like voting buttons (these allow recipients of the message to reply with a click of the mouse) and supplies you with the means to track the receipt of your message. You must be using the corporate email installation to take advantage of Voting buttons (see Lesson 3 for more information on the differences between the Outlook installations).

- Select the Use Voting Buttons check box to add the default choices (Approve and Reject) to your message. You can also add Yes and No choices or Yes, No, and Maybe choices. If you want to provide other choices, enter your own text in the text box.
- Select Tell Me When This Message Has Been Delivered to receive an email notification that the message has been received by the recipient.
- Select Tell Me When This Message Has Been Read to receive email confirmation that the message has been opened by the recipient.

DELIVERY OPTIONS

In addition to voting and tracking options, you can set certain delivery options, such as having replies sent to individuals you select. You can also choose a folder where a copy of the message will be saved, or schedule the time of the delivery. In the Delivery Options area of the Message Options dialog box, choose any of the following check boxes:

- Choose the Have Replies Sent To check box and specify in the text box the person to whom you want the replies sent. You can use the Select Names button to view the Address Book and choose a name if you want.
- Select the Save Sent Message To check box to save your message to the Sent Items folder by default. Or specify another folder to save the message in, using the Browse button and the resulting dialog box if necessary to locate the folder.
- Select the Do Not Deliver Before option to specify a delivery date. Click the down arrow in the text box beside the option to display a calendar on which you can select the day.

- Select the Expires After check box to include a day, date, and time of expiration. You can click the down arrow in the text box to display a calendar from which you can choose a date, or you can enter the date and time yourself.

CATEGORIES

Outlook enables you to assign messages to certain categories—such as Business, Goals, Hot Contacts, Phone Calls, and so on. You set the category for a message in the Categories dialog box.

Categories Categories offer a way of organizing messages to make them easier to find, sort, print, and manage. For example, to find all of the items in one category, choose Tools, Find Items. Click the More Choices tab, choose Categories, and check the category for which you're searching.

To assign a category, follow these steps:

1. In the Message Options dialog box, click the Categories button. The Categories dialog box appears (see Figure 10.2).

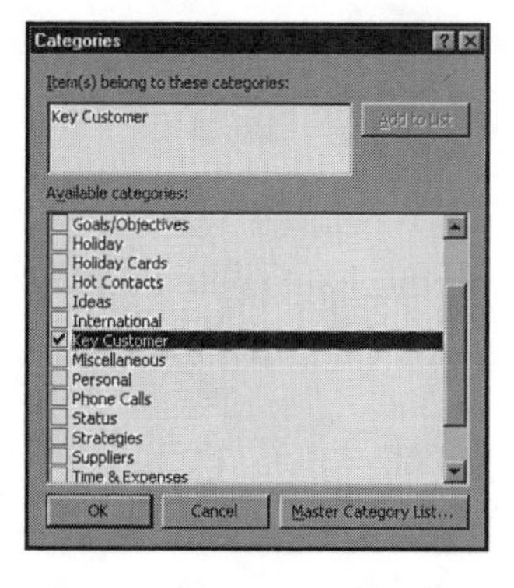

FIGURE 10.2 Organize your messages with categories.

2. To assign an existing category, select the category or categories that best suit your message from the Available Categories list. To assign a new category, enter a new category in the Item(s) Belong to These Categories text box, and then click the Add to List button.

3. Click OK to close the Categories dialog box and return to the Message Options dialog box.

When you have set all the options for the current message, click the Close button to close the Message Options box and return to the message window.

USING MESSAGE FLAGS

A message flag enables you to mark a message as important, either as a reminder for yourself or as a signal to the message's recipient. When you send a message flag, a red flag icon appears in the recipient's message list, and Outlook adds text at the top of the message telling which type of flag you are sending. In addition, you can add a due date to the flag, and that date appears at the top of the message.

The following list outlines the types of flags you can send in Outlook:

Call	No Response Necessary
Do not Forward	Read
Follow Up	Reply
For Your Information	Reply to All
Forward	Review

To use a message flag, follow these steps:

1. In the Message window, click Actions, Flag For Follow Up. The Flag for Follow Up dialog box appears (see Figure 10.3).

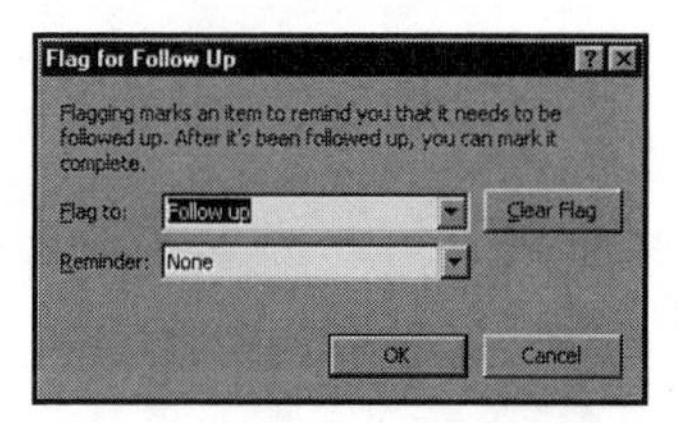

FIGURE 10.3 Flag a message to show its importance.

2. Click the Flag To drop-down arrow and choose the flag text you want to add to the message.
3. Click the Reminder drop-down arrow to enter a date in the text box.
4. Click OK to return to the Message window.

Figure 10.4 shows the Inbox and with a few flagged messages.

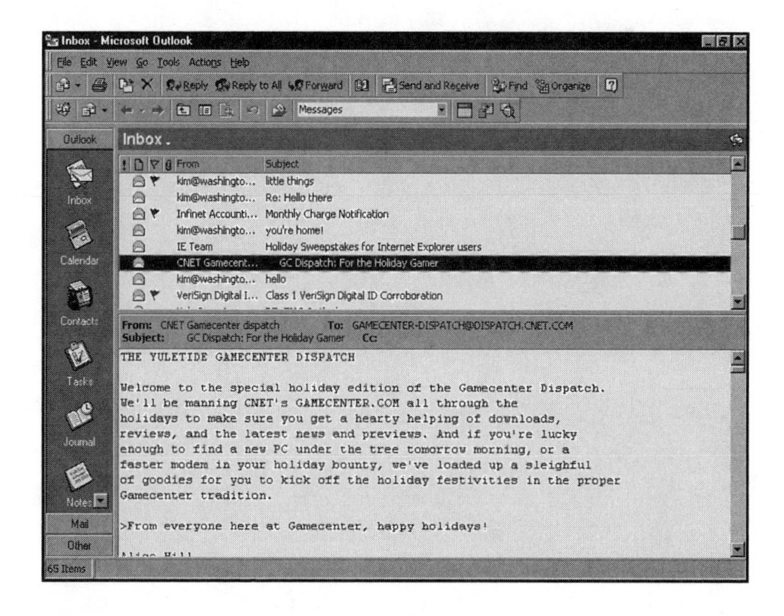

FIGURE 10.4 Flagged messages in the Inbox Folder. To view the type of flag attached, open the message.

View the Message Header You can view just the header of a message to allow you more message text room if you want to hide the Cc, Bcc, and Subject lines. Choose View, Message Header to show only the To text box and any flag text; select View, Message Header again to redisplay the Cc, Bcc, and Subject fields.

Marking messages with the Follow Up flag is a great way to remind yourself that you need to attend to a particular issue. Flagging messages for your email recipients helps them prioritize responses, so that you receive the needed reply within a particular time frame.

In this lesson, you learned to set options for messages and delivery, and for tracking messages. In the next lesson, you learn to attach items to messages.

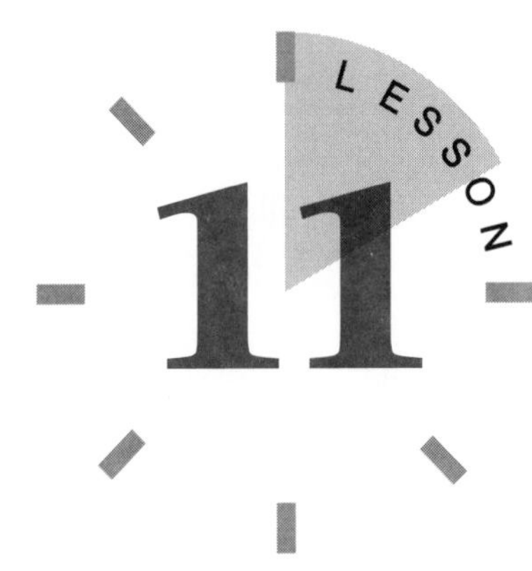

Attaching Files, Items, and Objects

In this lesson, you learn to attach a file and Outlook items to a message. You also learn how to insert an object in the other Outlook items, such as the calendar.

Attaching a File

You can attach any type of file to an Outlook message, which makes for a convenient way of sending your files over the network to your coworkers. You might send Word documents, Excel spreadsheets, a PowerPoint presentation, or any other document you create with your Windows 95/NT applications.

HTML Becomes Text If you send a message to someone who uses an email client that cannot read HTML messages, the message will appear as text. You must attach any pictures or other items to the message as an attachment if you want the user on the receiving end to view them.

When you send an attached file, it appears as an icon in a special attachment pane at the bottom of the message window. When the recipient gets the file, he or she can open it by double-clicking or save it for later use. However, the recipient must have the source program that you used to create the file on his or her computer. For instance, if you send a colleague a Microsoft Word file, he must have Microsoft Word in order to view the file he receives. Microsoft also supplies viewers for Microsoft Word and PowerPoint documents. These programs can be used to view Word and PowerPoint documents without having the full-blown software installed.

To attach a file to a message, follow these steps:

1. In the Message window, choose Insert, File or click the Insert File button on the toolbar. The Insert File dialog box appears (see Figure 11.1).

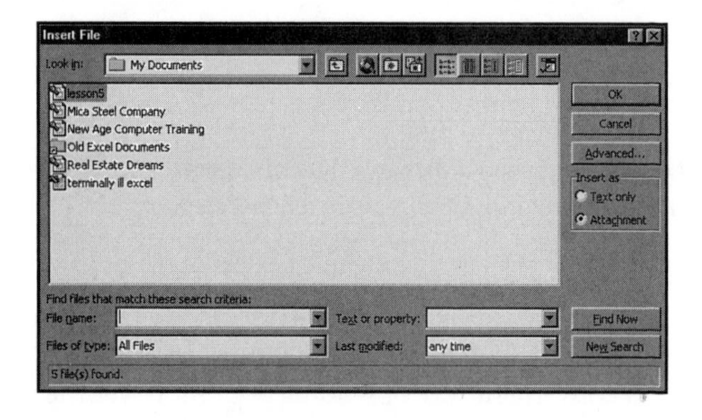

FIGURE 11.1 Select the file you want to attach to a message.

2. From the Look In drop-down list, choose the drive and folder that contains the file you want to attach.
3. Using the Files of Type drop-down list, choose the file type, such as Excel or Word.
4. Select the file you want to attach.
5. Click OK to insert the file into the message.

Figure 11.2 shows a file inserted as an attachment.

Large Files Take Time Sending an extremely large file can take a great deal of time depending on your connection speed. You may want to compress large files using products like WinZip or PKZip. These compression tools allow you to compress the size of attachments. However, the receivers of your messages will also need these tools if they are going to uncompress your attachments.

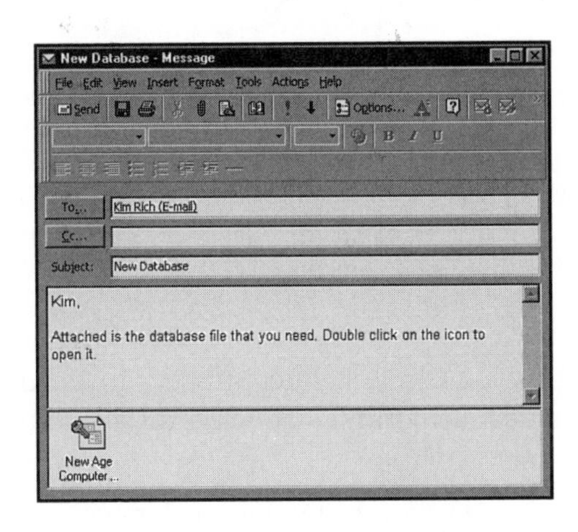

FIGURE 11.2 The recipient can double-click the icon to open the file.

UNDERSTANDING ATTACHMENT FORMAT TYPES

When you attach a file to an email message, it is coded in a special way so that the information remains intact when sent as part of the email message. Two of the most popular coding systems for attachments are *MIME* (Multipurpose Internet Mail Extension) and *UUEncoding*.

MIME This coding scheme places a header in the email message just before the information contained in the attached file. This lets the recipient's email client recognize which part of the sent message is the message text and which part is the attachment. Some online services and email packages have a problem decoding MIME attached files.

UUEncoding One of the most popular coding schemes. Most email packages can recognize and decode UUEncoded messages.

Check with Online Service Users Some online services, such as America Online, have restrictions on the size of an email that their mail server will accept. You should check with AOL or other service users before you send them files with large attachments to see if they have any special requirements.

Outlook enables you to select either MIME or UUEncoding as your default attachment format. To select the attachment coding system, follow these steps:

1. Click Tools, Options; the Options dialog box appears.
2. Click the Internet E-mail tab. Select either the MIME or UUENCODE radio button. UUENCODE is embraced by most email clients and should be your choice unless you know that you are specifically sending to individuals who use a client that embraces the MIME format.
3. After making your selection, click OK.

ATTACHING OUTLOOK ITEMS

In addition to attaching files from other programs, you can also attach an Outlook item to a message. An Outlook item can be any document saved in one of your personal folders, including a calendar, contacts, journal, notes, tasks, and so on. You can attach an Outlook item in the same manner you attach a file.

Follow these steps to attach an Outlook item:

1. In the Message window, choose Insert, Item. The Insert Item dialog box appears.
2. From the Look In list, choose the folder containing the item you want to include in the message.
3. Select from the items that appear in the Items list (see Figure 11.3). To select multiple adjacent items, hold down the Shift key and click the first and last desired items; to

select multiple nonadjacent items, hold down the Ctrl key and click the items.

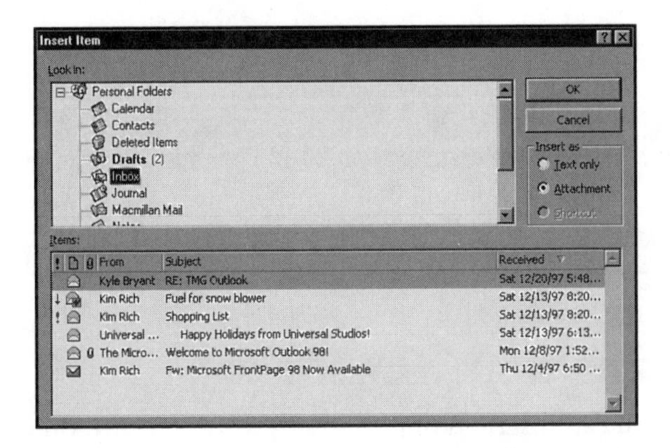

Figure 11.3 Select items from any folder in Outlook.

4. In the Insert As area, choose from the following option buttons:

   Text Only   Inserts the file as text into the message; if your file is not saved as an ASCII or other text-only file, do not use this option.

   Attachment   Inserts an icon representing the document. The actual file follows the message to the recipient; the recipient saves it as his or her own copy.

   Shortcut   Inserts a Windows 95 shortcut icon into the text. This option can only be used if the file is stored on a network drive from which the recipient can easily access it through a shortcut.

Text Only Is Only for Text! If you try to insert a file from Word, Excel, or another application as Text Only, you'll end up with a lot of "garbage" characters in the text. That's because these programs' files contain special formatting codes. The only time you will use Text Only is when you export the data from its native program into a text-only file first.

5. Click OK, and Outlook inserts the selected items in your message.

It Doesn't Work Without Outlook If the recipient doesn't have Outlook on his computer, he will not be able to view the attached item. If you know the recipient doesn't have the program, you'll need to cut and paste the data into the message or simply retype it.

INSERTING AN OBJECT

Just as you can insert an object—a spreadsheet, chart, drawing, presentation, media clip, clip art, WordArt, and so on—in any Windows application that supports *OLE*, you can also insert an object into your Outlook items, such as your calendar or task list. Inserting a file in a message, as discussed earlier, is the equivalent of inserting an object into one of the other Outlook items.

OLE (Object Linking and Embedding) A method of exchanging and sharing data between applications; OLE is supported by most Windows applications and all Microsoft programs.

You can insert an existing object into an Outlook item, or you can create an object within a message using the source application. For example, you could create an Excel chart within your message using Excel's features through OLE.

When you send a message with an attached object, the object travels with the message to the recipient. As long as the recipient has the application on his computer (or applicable viewer), he can open the object and view it.

For more information about OLE, see Lesson 22, "Sharing Data with Office Applications."

To attach an existing object to an appointment or task in the calendar, follow these steps:

1. Click the Calendar icon in the Outlook bar. Double-click an appointment or task on the task list. Position the insertion point in the appointment or task text box and choose Insert, Object. The Insert Object dialog box appears.

2. Choose the Create From File option (see Figure 11.4).

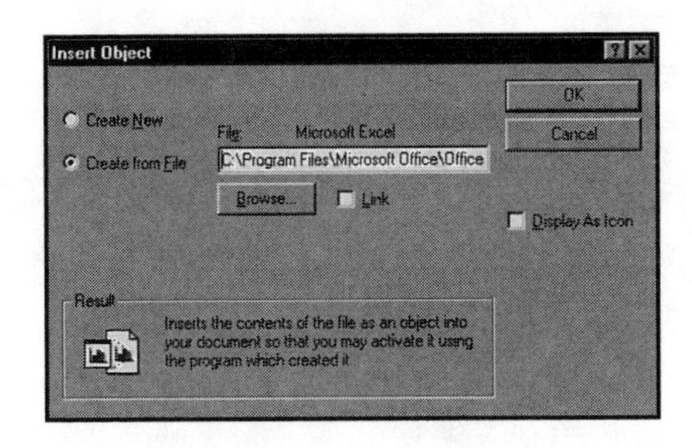

FIGURE 11.4 Insert an object to send with a message.

3. In the File text box, enter the path and the name of the file you want to insert. (You can use the Browse button and the resulting dialog box to find the file if you want.)

4. Click OK. Outlook inserts the object into the Outlook item.

To edit an object, double-click within the frame, and the source application opens from within Outlook. Note that you'll still see your Outlook item and Outlook toolbars; however, you'll also see tools associated with the object's source application, which you can use to edit the object. Figure 11.5 shows an Excel spreadsheet object within a task. Notice the Excel toolbar and icons added through OLE for use in editing the object.

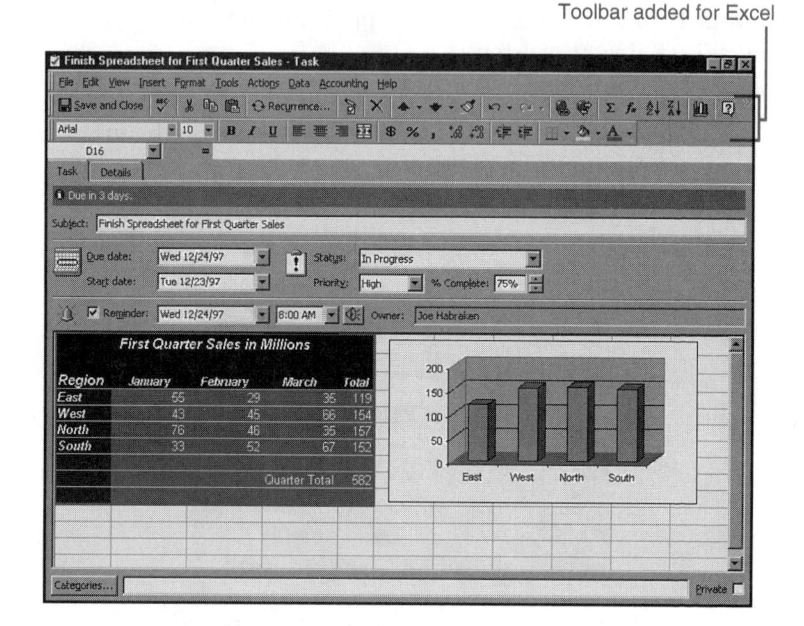

FIGURE 11.5 Edit the object from within your Outlook message.

When you double-click an object that is embedded in an Outlook item, you can resize the object to suit your needs. First select it, and a frame appears with eight small black boxes (called *handles*) on the corners and along the sides. To resize the object, position the mouse pointer over one of the black handles; the mouse pointer becomes a two-headed arrow. Click and drag the handle to resize the object.

In this lesson, you learned to attach a file and other items to a message. You also learned to insert an object in an Outlook item. In the next lesson, you learn to organize messages.

LESSON 12

ORGANIZING MESSAGES

In this lesson, you learn to save a draft, view sent items, create folders, and move items to the new folder.

SAVING A DRAFT

Suppose you start a message, but you are called away or need to do something else before you can finish it. You don't have to cancel the message and start over again later; you can save the message in the Draft folder and then open it later to complete it.

To save a draft, follow these steps:

1. In the Message window, click the Close button. A dialog box will appear asking if you want to save changes, as shown in Figure 12.1.

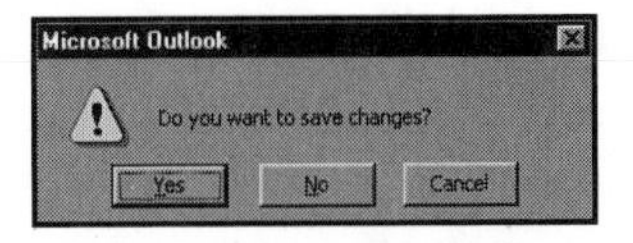

FIGURE 12.1 Click Yes to save the message in the Drafts folder for later completion.

2. Click Yes. Outlook places the current message in the Drafts Folder.

To open the message and continue working on it at another time, follow these steps:

1. Click the Drafts folder icon in the Outlook Bar, or choose Drafts from the Folders list.

2. Double-click the message to open it. At the top of the Message tab, you'll see a reminder that **This message has not been sent.**
3. Continue your work on the message. If you need to store it again before you're finished, click the Close button or choose File, Close. The message remains in the Drafts folder until you move it or send it.
4. When you're finished, click the Send button to send the message.

Create an Outlook Bar Icon for Drafts If you do not have a Drafts folder icon on the Outlook Bar, open the Folders list and right-click the Draft folder. On the shortcut menu that appears, select Add to Outlook Bar. An icon will appear on the Outlook Bar for the Drafts folder.

VIEWING SENT ITEMS AND CHANGING DEFAULTS

By default, Outlook saves a copy of all mail messages you send. It keeps these copies in the Sent Items folder, which is part of the Mail group of the Outlook Bar. You can view a list of sent items at any time, and you can open any message in that list to review its contents.

VIEWING SENT ITEMS

To view sent items, follow these steps:

1. In the Outlook Bar, choose the Mail group.

Save Time You can select the Sent Items folder from the Folder list instead of following steps 1–3.

2. If necessary, scroll to the Sent Items folder.

3. Click the Sent Items icon, and Outlook displays a list of the contents of that folder. Figure 12.2 shows the Sent Items list. All messages you send remain in the Sent Items folder until you delete or move them.

4. (Optional) To view a sent item, double-click it to open it. When you finish with it, click the Close (X) button.

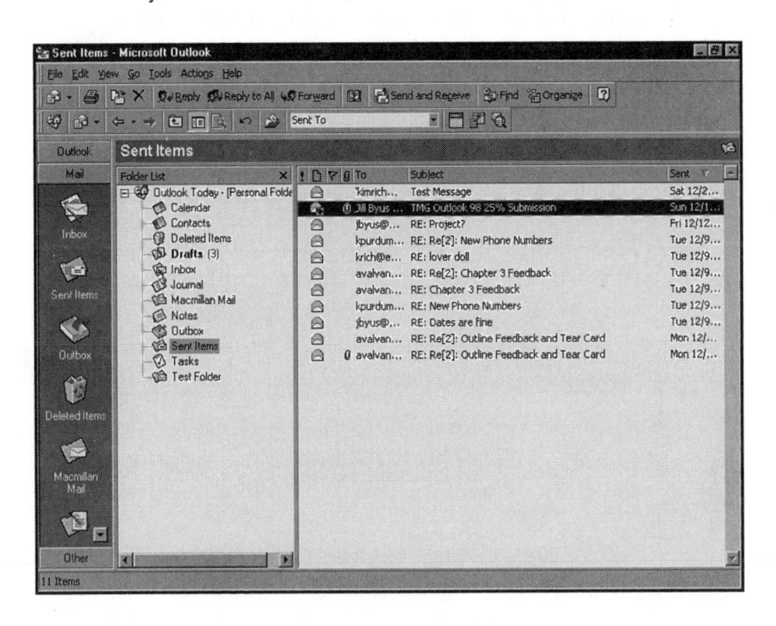

FIGURE 12.2 You can open any sent message by double-clicking it.

CHANGING DEFAULTS FOR SENT ITEMS

You can control whether or not Outlook saves copies of your sent messages (this is also true for unsent messages). To change the default setting for the Sent Items folder, follow these steps:

1. Choose Tools, Options, and the Options dialog box appears.

2. Click the E-mail Options button. The E-mail Options dialog box appears (see Figure 12.3). This dialog box allows you to toggle several email-related features on and off:

    - Close Original Message on Reply or Forward When this is checked, the message you currently have open will be closed when you reply to it or forward it. If this setting is unchecked, Outlook leaves the message window open.

- Save Copies of Messages in "Sent Items" Folder When this is checked, Outlook saves copies of all sent messages to the specified folder. (When the check box is empty, no copies of messages are saved automatically.)
- Automatically Save Unsent Messages When this is checked, Outlook saves your unfinished messages every three minutes, placing them in the Drafts folder. If you remove the check box from this feature, Drafts are not automatically saved.
- Close Original Message on Reply or Forward When this is checked, the message you currently have open will be closed when you reply to it or forward it. If this setting is unchecked, Outlook leaves the message window open.
- Display a Notification Message When New Mail Arrives When this is checked, a message appears in the Outlook window that new mail has arrived.

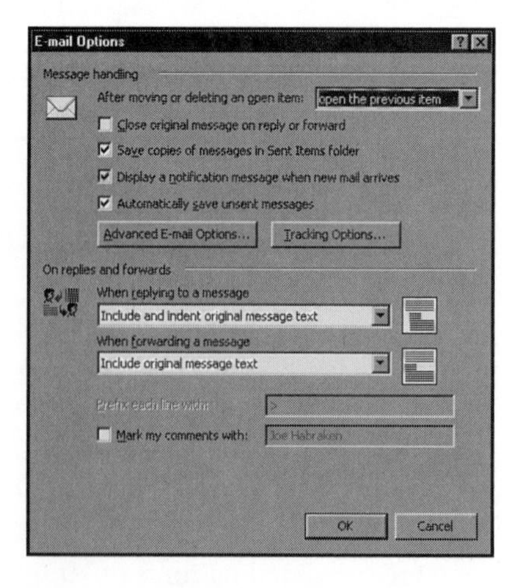

FIGURE 12.3 The E-mail Options dialog box gives you control over a number of features related to sending and receiving email messages.

The E-mail Options dialog box also gives you control over several other features related to the management of your email.

- Advanced E-mail Options button This button opens the Advanced E-mail Options dialog box. Most of the feature controls in the Advanced E-mail Options dialog box take the form of either check boxes or drop-down boxes. This dialog box allows you to control:

    The folder that unsent messages are sent to

    How often to save unsent messages

    Whether or not to save forwarded messages

    The default importance and sensitivity for outgoing messages

- Tracking Options button This button opens the Tracking Options dialog box where you can toggle on and off the following features:

    Tell me when all messages have been delivered.

    Tell me when all messages have been read.

    Delete receipts and blank responses after processing.

To close the E-Mail Options dialog box, click OK.

Too Much Mail! If you save all the mail you receive and send, you may accumulate so much mail that you run the risk of running out of disk space. You can and should periodically delete mail from the Sent Items folder by selecting the mail and pressing the Delete key; you'll also need to remove the deleted mail from the Deleted Items folder. See Lesson 7, "Managing Mail," for more information. Alternatively, you can create an archive file of the messages you've sent. The archive enables you to save items on disk or elsewhere on the system. See Lesson 23, "Archiving Items," for details.

CREATING FOLDERS

You'll probably want to organize your mail in various folders to make storing items and finding them more efficient. You can create folders within Outlook that make it easier to manage your mail and other items in Outlook.

To create a folder, follow these steps:

1. Choose File, New, Folder. The Create New Folder dialog box appears (see Figure 12.4).

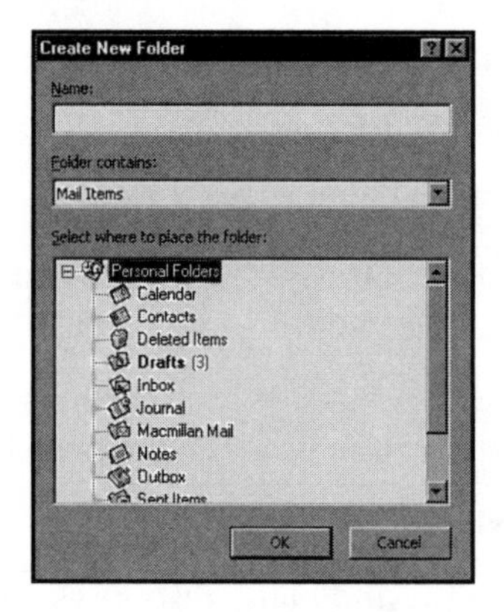

FIGURE 12.4 Create folders to organize your mail and other items.

2. In the Name text box, enter a name for the folder.
3. Click the Folder Contains drop-down arrow, and choose the type of items the folder will store—Mail, Appointments, Contact, Journal, Note, or Task.
4. Double-click the folder in which you want to create the new folder. You can, for example, make the new folder a subfolder of Personal Folders so that it appears in lists with all of the Outlook folders. Or you might want to make it a subfolder of Sent Mail.

5. Click OK to close the dialog box. A message box will appear asking if you want a shortcut icon created for the new folder on the Outlook Bar. Click Yes if you want the shortcut.

The new folder appears on the Outlook Bar and in the Folder List.

Add Folder Later Even if you choose not to add the folder to the Outlook Bar when you create the folder, you can add it later. You simply right-click the folder in the folder list and select Add to Outlook Bar from the shortcut menu that appears.

I Want to Delete a Folder! If you added a folder by accident or you change your mind about a folder you've added, you can delete it from Outlook. To delete a folder, select it and then choose File, Folder, Delete *foldername*. You also can rename, move, and/or copy the folder using the commands in the secondary menu that appears when you choose File, Folder.

MOVING ITEMS TO ANOTHER FOLDER

You can move items from one folder in Outlook to another; for example, you can create a folder to store all messages pertaining to a specific account or report. You can easily move those messages to the new folder and open them later for reference purposes. You also can forward, reply, copy, delete, and archive any items you move from one folder to another.

To move an item to another folder, follow these steps:

1. From the Inbox, or any Outlook folder, open the message you want to move.
2. Choose Edit, Move to Folder. The Move Items dialog box appears (see Figure 12.5).

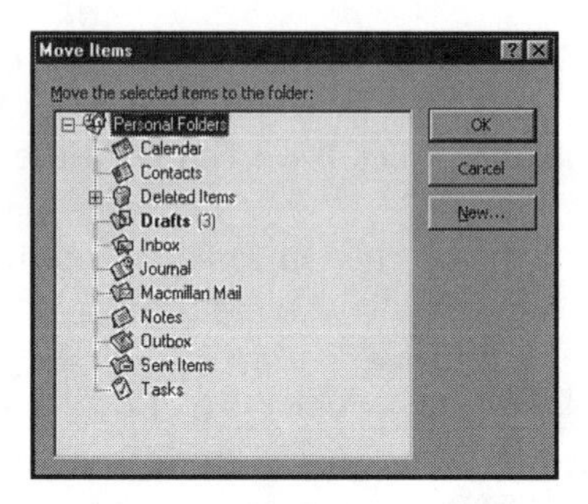

FIGURE 12.5 Choose the folder in which you want to store the message.

3. In the list of folders, select the folder to which you want to move the message.
4. Choose OK. When you close the message, Outlook stores it in the designated folder.

Quick Move You can quickly move an unopened message by dragging it from the open folder in which it resides to any folder icon in the Outlook Bar.

You can open the message at any time by opening the folder from the Outlook Bar and double-clicking the message. After opening it, you can forward, send, print, or otherwise manipulate the message as you would any message.

Manage Messages with the Organizer Tool and Rules Wizard Two great tools for helping you manage your messages are the Organize tool and the Rules Wizard. Both features are covered in Lesson 7, "Managing Mail."

In this lesson, you learned to save a draft, view sent items, create folders, and move items to a folder. In the next lesson, you'll learn to use the Calendar.

LESSON 13

USING THE CALENDAR

In this lesson, you learn to navigate the Calendar, create appointments, and save appointments.

NAVIGATING THE CALENDAR

You can use Outlook's Calendar to schedule appointments and create a to-do list; if necessary, Outlook can also remind you of appointments and daily or weekly tasks. You can schedule appointments months in advance, move appointments, cancel appointments, and so on. And the Calendar makes it easy to identify the days on which you have appointments.

To open the Outlook Calendar, click the Calendar icon in the Outlook Bar, or select the Calendar folder from the Folder list. Figure 13.1 shows the Calendar in Outlook.

Outlook provides multiple ways for you to move around in the Calendar and view specific dates:

- Scroll through the Appointment pane to view the time of an appointment.
- In the monthly calendar pane, click the left and right arrows next to the names of the months to go backward and forward one month at a time.

Changing Calendar Views You can change to different views of the calendar by clicking the Current View drop-down arrow on the Advanced Toolbar. Views including Active Appointments, Recurring Appointments, and By Category are available.

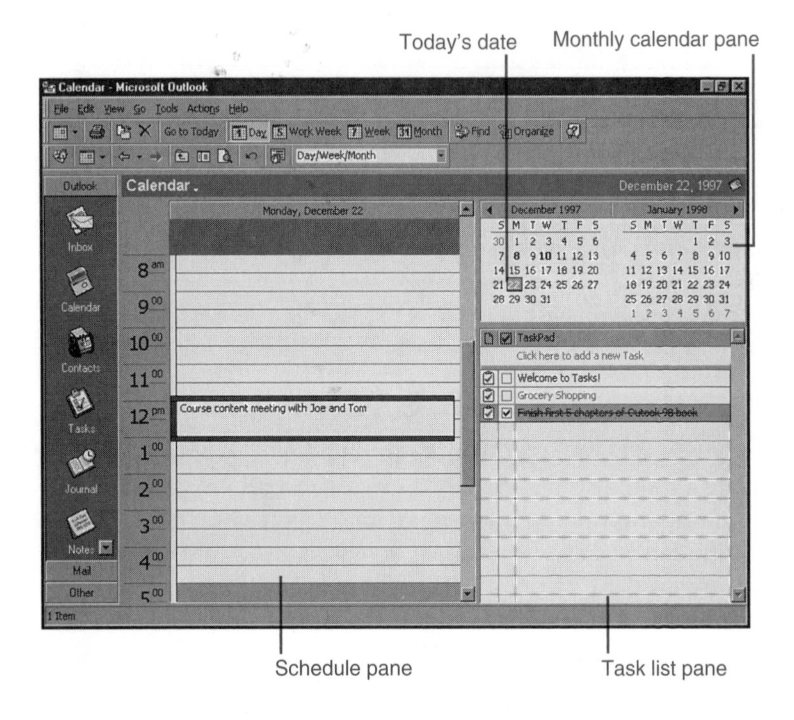

FIGURE 13.1 You can view all appointments and tasks at a glance.

- In the monthly calendar pane, click a date to display that date in the schedule pane.
- To switch to a different month in the schedule pane, click the current month in the monthly calendar pane, and select the name of the month from the shortcut list.
- To view a week or selected days in the schedule pane, select the days in the monthly calendar pane.
- To add a task to the Task list, click where you see **Click here to add a new Task**.
- Use the scroll bars for the Task list pane to view additional tasks, if necessary.

Change the Date Quickly To quickly go to today's date or to a specific date without searching through the monthly calendar pane, right-click in the schedule pane and choose either Go To Today or Go To Date.

CREATING AN APPOINTMENT

You can create an appointment on any day well past the year 2000 using the Outlook Calendar. When you create an appointment, you can add the subject, location, starting time, category, and even an alarm to remind you ahead of time.

Follow these steps to create an appointment:

1. In the monthly calendar pane, select the month and the date for which you want to create an appointment.
2. In the schedule pane, double-click next to the time at which the appointment is scheduled to begin. The Untitled - Appointment dialog box appears, with the Appointment tab displayed (see Figure 13.2).

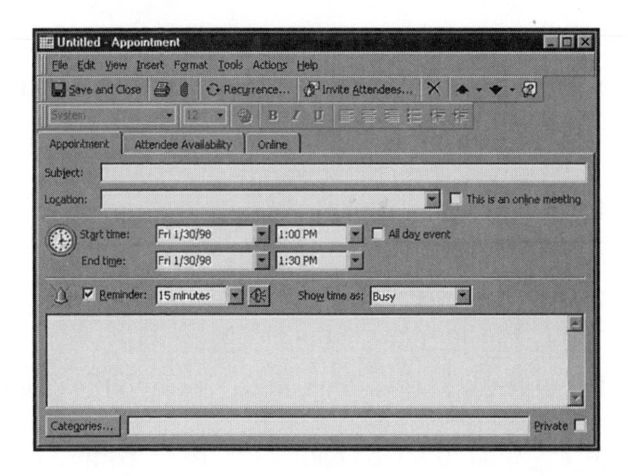

FIGURE 13.2 Enter all the details you need when scheduling an appointment.

3. Enter the subject of the appointment in the Subject text box (you can use a person's name, a topic, or other information).
4. In the Location text box, enter the meeting place or other text that will help you identify the meeting when you see it in your calendar.
5. Enter dates and times in the Start Time and End Time boxes (or click the drop-down arrows and select the dates and times).

Autodate It! You can use Outlook's Autodate feature: enter a text phrase such as "next Friday" or "noon" in the date and time text boxes, and Outlook figures out the date for you.

6. Select the Reminder check box and enter the amount of time before the appointment that you want to be notified. If you want to set an audio alarm, click the alarm bell button and select a specific sound for Outlook to play as your reminder.
7. From the Show Time As drop-down list, choose how you want to display the scheduled time on your calendar.
8. In the large text box near the bottom of the Appointment tab, enter any text that you want to include, such as text to identify the appointment, reminders for materials to take, and so on.
9. Click the Categories button and assign a category (or categories) to the appointment.
10. Click the Save and Close button to return to the calendar.

The Attendee Availability tab enables you to schedule a meeting with coworkers and enter the meeting on your Calendar. See Lesson 14, "Planning a Meeting," for more information.

SCHEDULING A RECURRING APPOINTMENT

Suppose you have an appointment that comes around every week or month, or that otherwise occurs on a regular basis. Instead of scheduling every individual occurrence of the appointment, you can schedule that appointment in your calendar as a recurring appointment.

To schedule a recurring appointment, follow these steps:

1. In the Calendar folder, choose the Actions menu, then New Recurring Appointment. The Appointment dialog box appears, and then the Appointment Recurrence dialog box appears on top of the Appointment dialog box (as shown in Figure 13.3).

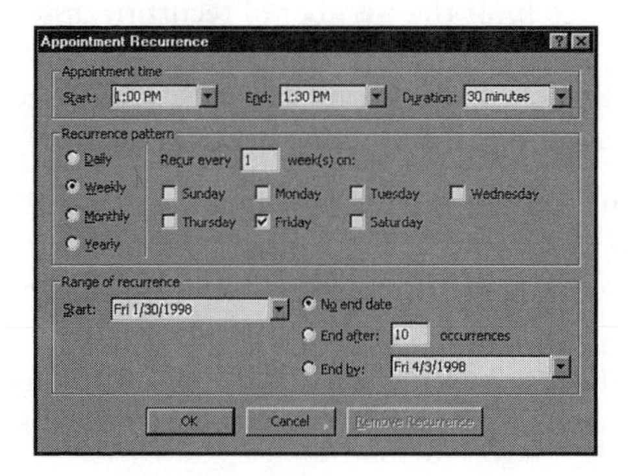

FIGURE 13.3 Schedule a recurring appointment once, and Outlook fills in the appointment for you throughout the Calendar.

2. In the Appointment Time area, enter the Start, End, and Duration times for the appointment.
3. In the Recurrence Pattern area, indicate the frequency of the appointment—Daily, Weekly, Monthly, or Yearly. After you select one of these options, the rest of the Recurrence Pattern area changes.

4. Enter the day and month, as well as any other options in the Recurrence Pattern area that are specific to your selection in Step 3.

5. In the Range of Recurrence area, enter appropriate time limits according to these guidelines:

    - Start Choose the date on which the recurring appointments will begin.
    - No End Date Choose this option if the recurring appointments are not on a limited schedule.
    - End After Choose this option and enter the number of appointments if there is a specific limit to the recurring appointments.
    - End By Choose this option and enter an ending date to limit the number of recurring appointments.

6. Click OK to close the Appointment Recurrence dialog box. The Appointment dialog box appears.

7. Fill in the Appointment dialog box as described previously in this lesson. When you finish, click the Save and Close button to return to the Calendar. The recurring appointment appears in your calendar on the specified date and time. A recurring appointment contains a double-arrow icon to indicate that it is recurring.

Recurring Meetings You can schedule a recurring meeting by clicking the Actions menu and then selecting New Recurring Meeting. The Appointment dialog box and Recurrence dialog box will both be opened by this Calendar menu selection. Meetings are covered in Lesson 14.

PLANNING EVENTS

In the Outlook Calendar, an *event* is any activity that lasts at least 24 hours, such as a trade show or a conference. You can plan an event in the Calendar program to block off larger time slots than you would for normal appointments. In addition, you can schedule recurring events.

To schedule an event, choose Actions, New All Day Event. The Event dialog box appears; it looks very much like the New Appointment dialog box. Fill in the Subject, Location, Start Time, and End Time text boxes. Make sure the All Day Event check box is checked (that's the only difference between an Event and an Appointment). Click the Save and Close button to return to the Outlook Calendar. The appointment appears in gray at the beginning of the day for which you scheduled the event.

To schedule a recurring event, open a New All Day Event window and fill in the information as described earlier. To make the event recurring, click the Recurrence button in the Event window. The Event Recurrence dialog box will open; fill in the appropriate information and click OK. Complete the information in the Event window, and then click the Save and Close button.

To edit an event or a recurring event, double-click the event in your calendar. As with a mail message or appointment, Outlook opens the event window so you can change times, dates, or other details of the event.

In this lesson, you learned to navigate the Calendar, create appointments, and save appointments. In the next lesson, you will learn to plan a meeting.

LESSON 14

PLANNING A MEETING

In this lesson, you learn to schedule a meeting, enter attendees for a planned meeting, set the meeting date and time, and invite others to the meeting.

SCHEDULING A MEETING

Outlook provides methods by which you can plan the time and date of a meeting, identify the subject and location of the meeting, invite others to attend the meeting, and identify resources that will be needed for the meeting. You use the Calendar folder to plan and schedule meetings.

Meeting In Outlook, a meeting is an appointment to which you invite people and resources.

Attendees The people who will be attending your meeting.

Resources Any equipment you use in your meeting, such as a computer, slide projector, or even the room itself.

To plan a meeting, follow these steps:

1. Click the icon for the Calendar folder, and then choose Actions, Plan a Meeting. The Plan A Meeting dialog box appears (see Figure 14.1).

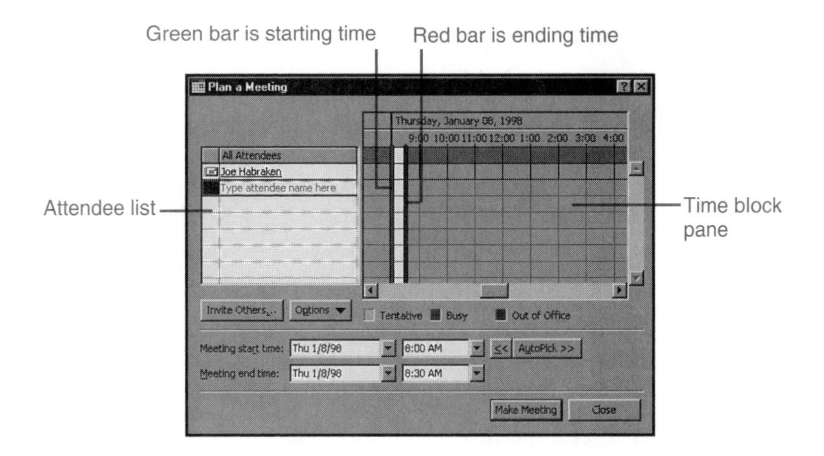

FIGURE 14.1 Choose the date and time of your meeting as well as the attendees.

2. To enter the names of the attendees, click in the All Attendees list where it says **Type Attendee Name Here**. Enter the name and press Enter. Continue adding new names as necessary.

Invite More People You can click the Invite Others button to choose names from your Personal Address Book or the Outlook Address Book.

3. To set a date for the meeting, open the leftmost Meeting Start Time drop-down list and select the date from the calendar, or just type the date in the text box. The ending date (in the Meeting End Time drop-down list) automatically shows the same date you set in the Meeting Start Time date box; you can change the End Time date if you want.

4. To set a start time for the meeting, do one of the following:

   - Open the Meeting Start Time drop-down list, and select the time.

- Type a time in the text box.
- Drag the green bar in the time block pane of the dialog box to set the start time.

5. To set an end time for the meeting, do one of the following:
    - Open the Meeting End Time drop-down list, and select the end time.
    - Type a time in the text box.
    - Drag the red bar in the time block pane of the dialog box to change the ending time of the meeting.

After you select the date and time for the meeting, you will notice that the time grid to the right of each attendee name shows the currently scheduled appointments that they have on the day of the meeting. The times blocked out in each attendee's grid are based on appointments and meetings in their Outlook Calendar. Outlook is able to check your corporate network and check attendee availability by using their calendars. If you have a conflict between your meeting time and an attendee's appointment, you can adjust the time of your meeting and avoid availability conflicts.

6. When you finish planning the meeting, click the Make Meeting button. The Meeting window appears (see Figure 14.2), from which you can refine the meeting details, as described in the next section.

Use AutoPick to Shift Meeting Time Frame You can click the AutoPick decrease or increase buttons to shift the meeting time (including the beginning and ending) to a half hour earlier or later respectively. Each time you click AutoPick, the meeting shifts another half hour.

WORKING OUT MEETING DETAILS

After you plan a meeting, Outlook enables you to send invitations, identify the subject of the meeting, and specify the meeting's location. You enter these details in the Meeting dialog box.

When you schedule a meeting, you finish by clicking the Make Meeting button in the Plan A Meeting dialog box. When you do that, Outlook displays the Meeting dialog box with the Appointment tab in front (see Figure 14.2).

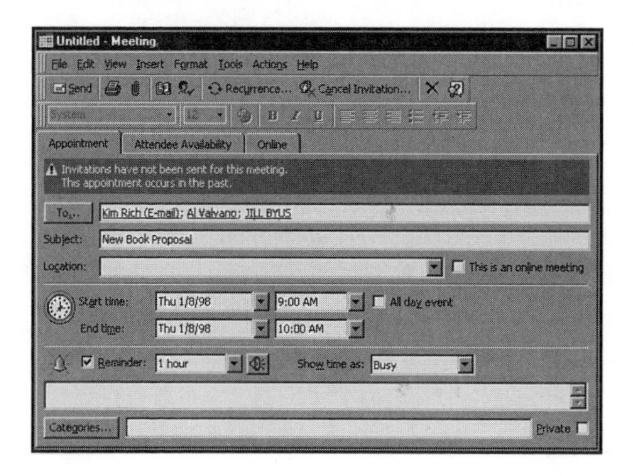

FIGURE 14.2 Specify the details related to the meeting in the Appointment tab of the Meeting dialog box.

Follow these steps to specify meeting details for a meeting you've already scheduled.

1. If you did not list the attendees in the Plan A Meeting dialog box, either click in the To text box and enter the names of the people you want to attend the meeting, or click the To button to select the attendees from an address book or Contact list.
2. In the Subject text box, enter a subject for the meeting.
3. In the Location text box, enter a location for the meeting.

4. (Optional) You can change the starting and ending dates and/or times in the Appointment tab. You also can choose the Attendee Availability tab to view the meeting in a format similar to that of the Plan A Meeting dialog box; make any changes to attendees, time, dates, and so on in the Attendee Availability tab.

5. (Optional) Select the Reminder check box, and enter a time for Outlook to sound an alarm to remind you of the meeting.

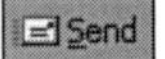

6. (Optional) Enter any special text you want to send the attendees in the text box provided.

About the Online Tab The Meeting dialog box contains a tab marked Online. This tab is used to set up a meeting online using Microsoft NetMeeting. Scheduling an online meeting is really no different than scheduling a face-to-face meeting; you follow the same scheduling steps outlined in this lesson. An online meeting, however, requires that you specify a Directory Server that will be used to connect the participants. Using NetMeeting is covered in Lesson 25, "Outlook and the Internet."

7. When you're ready to send the invitations to the meeting, click the Send button. Close the Meeting window by choosing File, Close.

When you send an invitation, you're sending an email that requests the presence of the recipient at the meeting. The recipient can reply to your message, save your message, and forward or delete the message, just as he can with any other email message. If you want the recipient to reply, choose Appointment, Request Responses, and the recipients will be prompted to reply to your invitation.

An Invitation Mistake To cancel an invitation after you've sent it, choose Appointment, Cancel Invitation.

INVITING OTHERS TO THE MEETING

If you need to add names to your attendees list—either while you're planning the meeting or at some later date—you can use your personal address book, the Outlook address book, and/or your Contact list to find the names of the people you want to invite. Additionally, you can choose whether to make the meeting required or optional for each person you invite.

To invite others to the meeting, follow these steps:

1. In either the Plan A Meeting dialog box or the Attendee Available tab of the Meeting dialog box, click the Invite Others button. The Select Attendees and Resources dialog box appears, as shown in Figure 14.3.

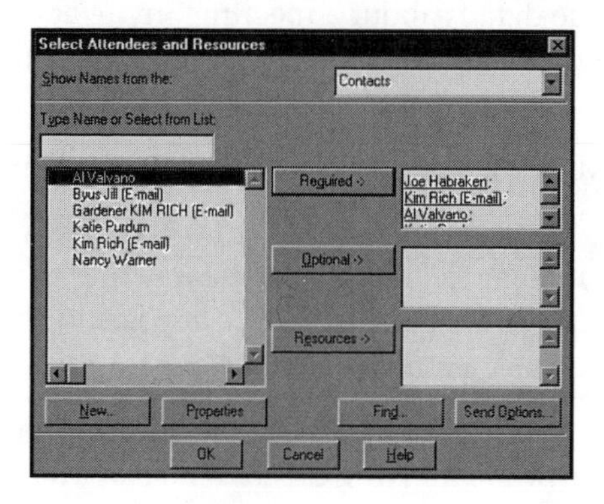

FIGURE 14.3 Use the address books to specify attendees to your meeting.

2. Open the Show Names From The drop-down list, and choose either Personal Address Book or Contacts.

3. To add a new name to a list, click the New button, and then enter the name, email address, phone numbers, and other pertinent information about the name you're adding to the list.

4. Select any name in the list on the left side of the dialog box and click the Required or Optional button to specify attendance requirements.

Reserve Resources Click the New button to add resources to the list; then notify the person who is in charge of those resources of your meeting.

5. Click OK to close the dialog box and add any attendees to your list.

EDITING A MEETING

You can edit the details about a meeting, invite additional people, or change the date and time of the meeting at any time by opening the Meeting dialog box.

To open the Meeting dialog box and edit the meeting, follow these steps:

1. In the Calendar folder, choose the meeting date in the monthly calendar pane. The date appears in the schedule pane, and the meeting is blocked out for the time period you specified, as shown in Figure 14.4.

2. Double-click the meeting block to display the Meeting dialog box. You can edit anything in the Appointment or Meeting Planner tabs.

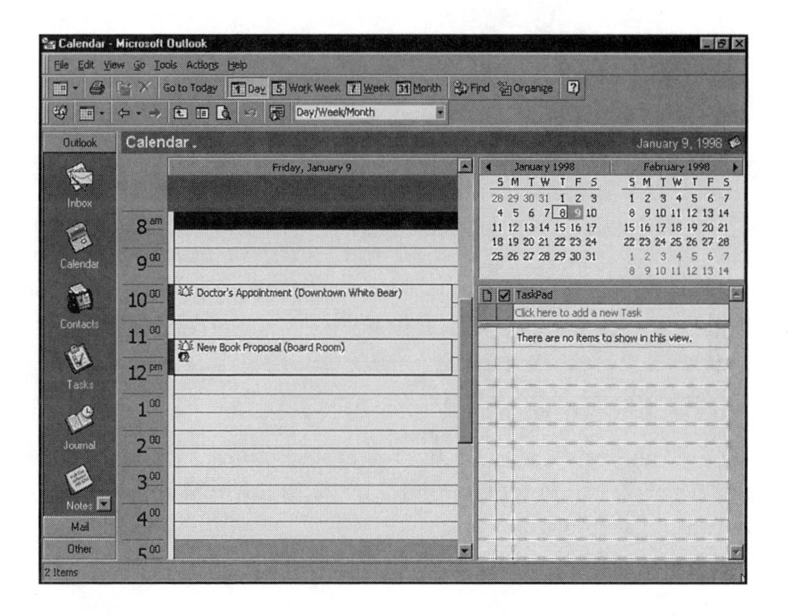

FIGURE 14.4 Select the meeting you want to edit from within the Calendar.

Any Responses? Choose the Show Attendee Status option in the Attendee Availability tab of the Meeting dialog box to see if the people you invited to the meeting have responded to your invitation.

3. When you're done, choose File, Close to close the Meeting dialog box. If you've made changes to the meeting specifics, you should also send a message to your attendees to notify them of the change.

In this lesson, you learned to schedule a meeting, enter attendees for a planned meeting, set the meeting time, and invite others to the meeting. In the next lesson, you'll learn to create a contacts list.

LESSON 15

Creating a Contacts List

In this lesson, you learn to create and view a Contacts list, and to send mail to someone on your Contacts list.

Creating a New Contact

You use the Contacts folder to create, store, and utilize your Contacts list. You can enter any or all of the following information about each contact:

- Name
- Job title
- Company name
- Address (Street, City, State, ZIP, and Country)
- Phone (business, home, business fax, mobile)
- Email address
- Web page address
- Comments, notes, or descriptions
- Categories

Contact In Outlook, a contact is any person or company for which you've entered a name, address, phone number, or other information. You can communicate with a contact in Outlook by sending an email message, scheduling a meeting, sending a letter, and so on.

You also can edit the information at any time, add new contacts, or delete contacts from the list. To open the Contacts folder and create a new contact, follow these steps:

1. To open the Contacts folder, click the Contacts shortcut on the Outlook Bar. The Contacts folder opens.
2. To create a new contact, select Actions, New Contact, or simply click the New Contact button on the Standard or Advanced toolbar. The Contact dialog box appears, with the General tab displayed (see Figure 15.1).

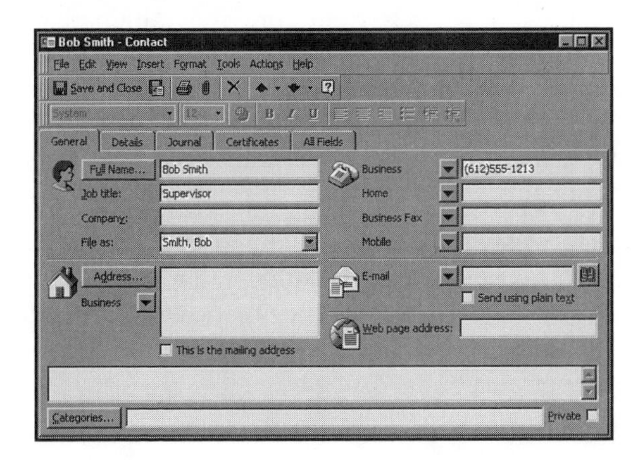

FIGURE 15.1 You can enter as much or as little information about each contact as you need.

3. Enter the contact's name in the Name text box. If you want to add more detailed information for the name, click the Full Name button to display the Check Full Name dialog box, and then enter the contact's title and full name (including first, middle, and last names) and any suffix you want to include. Click OK to close the Check Full Name dialog box and return to the Contact dialog box.
4. Press the Tab key and then enter the client's company name and job title. This information is optional.
5. In the File As drop-down box, enter or select the method by which you want to file your contact's names. You can choose last name first or first name first, or you can enter your own filing system, such as by company or state.

Keep It Simple The default filing method for contacts is last name first, which makes it easy to quickly find the contact when you need it.

6. Enter the address in the Address box and choose whether the address is Business, Home, or Other. Alternatively, you can click the Address button to enter the street, city, state, ZIP code, and country in specified areas instead of all within the text block. You can add a second address (say, the Home address) if you want. Address information is optional.
7. In the Phone drop-down lists, choose the type of phone number—Business, Callback, Car, Home Fax, ISDN, Pager, and so on—and then enter the number. You can enter up to 19 numbers in each of the four drop-down boxes in the Phone area of the dialog box.
8. You can enter up to three email addresses in the E-mail text box; in the Web Page Address text box, enter the address for the company or contact's URL on the World Wide Web.

If you have more than one email address for a contact When you place more than one phone number or email address in a drop-down list, the first number or address in the list serves as the default. For example, when emailing a contact, the first email address in the list will serve as the default and be placed in the To box on the new message. If you want to use a different email address for the contact, double-click the contact's name in the Message To box, and select one of the other email addresses in the contact's Properties box. When you want to call a contact for whom you have multiple numbers, a drop-down list appears in the New Call dialog box and allows you to choose the appropriate number.

URL Stands for Uniform Resource Locator, and simply means the address for a Web page on the World Wide Web. A typical URL would be written **http://www.*companyname*.com**, such as **http://www.mcp.com**.

9. In the comment text box, enter any descriptions, comments, or other pertinent information you want. Then select or enter a category to classify the contact.
10. After you have completed entering the new contact information, click the Save and Close button to return to the Contacts folder. You can also save the new contact by opening the File menu and choosing one of the following commands:

    Save Saves the record and closes the Contact dialog box.

    Save and New Saves the record and clears the Contact dialog box so you can enter a new contact.

You can edit the information about a contact at any time by double-clicking the contact's name in the Contacts list; this displays the contact's information window. Alternatively, you can click within the information listed below a contact's name (such as the phone number or address) to position the insertion point in the text, and then delete or enter text. Press Enter to complete the modifications you've made and move to the next contact in the list.

VIEWING THE CONTACTS LIST

By default, you see the contacts in an Address Cards view. The information you see displays the contact's name and other data such as addresses and phone numbers. The contact's company name, job title, and comments, however, are not displayed by default. Figure 15.2 shows the Contacts list in the default Address Cards view.

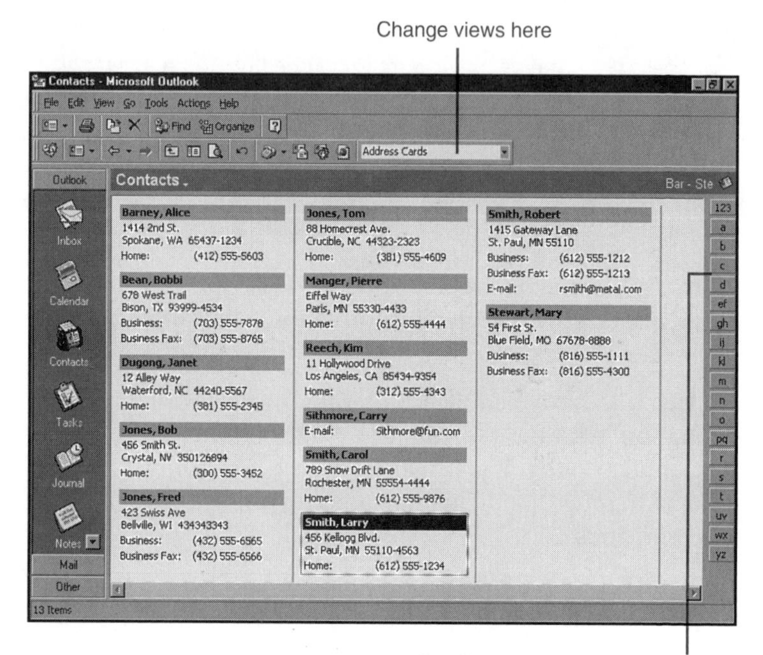

FIGURE 15.2 View your contacts in Address Cards view.

You can use the horizontal scroll bar to view more contacts, or you can click a letter in the index to display contacts beginning with that letter in the first column of the list.

Do I Save View Settings? Depending on the changes you make to a view, Outlook might display the Save View Settings dialog box to ask if you want to save the view settings before you switch to a different view. If you choose to save the current settings, Outlook lets you name the view and adds that view to the Current View list. If you choose to discard the current settings, your modifications to the view will be lost. If you choose to update the view, your modifications are saved with that view.

You can change how you view the contacts in the list by choosing one of these options from the Current View drop-down list on the Standard toolbar:

- **Address Cards** Displays File As names (last name first, first name last, and so on), addresses, and phone numbers of the contacts, depending on the amount of information you've entered in a card format.
- **Detailed Address Cards** Displays File As name, full name, job title, company, addresses, phone numbers, email addresses, categories, and comments in a card format.
- **Phone List** Displays full name, job title, company, File As name, department, phone numbers, and categories in a table, organizing each entry horizontally in rows and columns.
- **By Category** Displays contacts in rows by categories. The information displayed is the same as what's displayed in a phone list.
- **By Company** Displays contacts in rows, grouped by their company. The information displayed is the same as what's displayed in a phone list.
- **By Location** Displays contacts grouped by country. The information displayed is the same as what's displayed in a phone list.
- **By Follow Up Flag** Displays contacts grouped by follow-up flags. The view also displays the due date for the follow-up that you specified when you marked the contact with a flag.

COMMUNICATING WITH A CONTACT

You can send messages to any of your contacts, arrange meetings, assign tasks, or even send a letter to a contact from within Outlook. To communicate with a contact, make sure you're in the

Contacts folder. You do not need to open the specific contact's information window to perform any of the following procedures.

SENDING MESSAGES

To send a message to a contact, you must make sure you've entered an email address in the General tab of the Contact dialog box for that particular contact. If Outlook cannot locate the mailing address, it displays a message dialog box (see Figure 15.3).

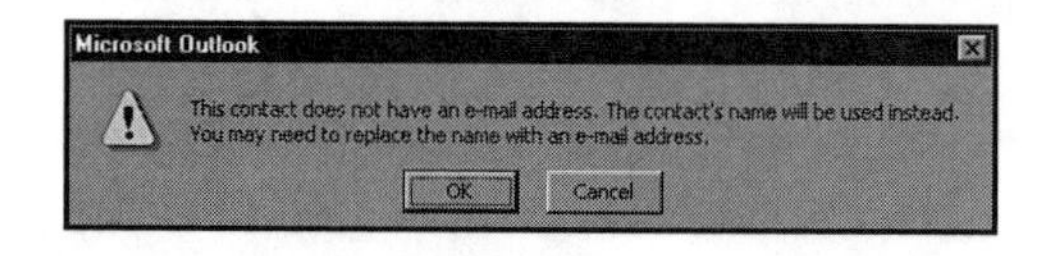

FIGURE 15.3 Outlook cannot send the email until you complete the address in the New Message dialog box.

To send a message from the Contacts folder, select the contact and choose Actions, New Message to Contact. In the Untitled - Message dialog box, enter the subject and message and set any options you want. When you're ready to send the message, click the Send button. For more information about sending mail, see Lesson 9, "Creating Mail."

SCHEDULING A MEETING WITH A CONTACT

To schedule a meeting with a contact, the contact must have a valid email address. If no address is listed for the contact, Outlook notifies you with a message box and enables you to enter an address within the message dialog box. If the listed address is not found, Outlook responds with the Check Names dialog box, as described in the previous section.

To schedule a meeting with a contact, select the contact and choose Actions, New Meeting with Contact. The Untitled - Meeting dialog box appears. Enter the subject, location, time and date, and other information you need to schedule the meeting, and then notify the contact by sending an invitation. For more information about scheduling meetings, see Lesson 14, "Planning a Meeting."

ASSIGNING A TASK TO A CONTACT

Tasks are assigned through email. Therefore, you must enter a valid email address for the contact before you can assign him or her a task.

To assign a task to a contact, select the contact and choose Actions, New Task for Contact. The Task dialog box appears. Enter the subject, due date, status, and other information, and then send the task to the contact. For detailed information about assigning tasks, see Lesson 16, "Creating a Task List."

SENDING A LETTER TO A CONTACT

Outlook uses the Microsoft Word Letter Wizard to help you create a letter to send to a contact. Within the Word Wizard, you follow directions as they appear onscreen to complete the text of the letter.

To send a letter to the contact, select the contact in the Contact folder and choose Actions, New Letter to Contact. Word opens the Letter Wizard onscreen. The Letter Wizard helps you format and complete the letter (see Figure 15.4). You can click the Office Assistant button if you need additional help. All you have to do is follow the directions and make your choices.

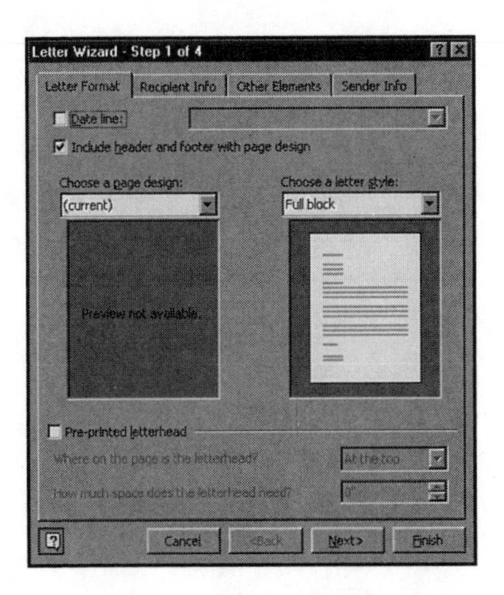

FIGURE 15.4 Use Word's Letter Wizard to create a letter to a contact.

In this lesson, you learned to create a Contacts list, view the list, and send mail to someone on your Contacts list. In the next lesson, you learn to create a task list.

LESSON 16

Creating a Task List

In this lesson, you learn to enter a task and record statistics about the task.

Entering a Task

You can use the Tasks folder to create and manage your task list. You can list due dates, status, and priorities, and even set reminder alarms so you don't forget to perform certain tasks. To enter the Tasks folder, click the Task shortcut in the Outlook Bar.

Task List A task list is simply a list of things you must do to complete your work, such as plan for a meeting, arrange an event, and so on. Various tasks might include making a phone call, writing a letter, printing a spreadsheet, or making airline reservations.

To enter a task, follow these steps:

1. In the Tasks folder, choose Actions, New Task or click the New Task button on the toolbar. The Untitled - Task dialog box appears (see Figure 16.1).
2. In the Task tab, enter the subject of the task in the Subject box.
3. Enter a date on which the task should be complete, or click the down arrow to open the Due date drop-down calendar, and then choose a due date.
4. Enter a start date, or click the down arrow to open the Start date drop-down calendar, and then choose a starting date.

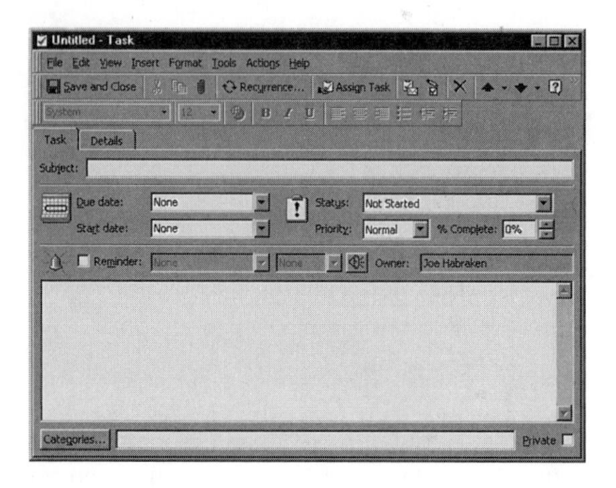

FIGURE 16.1 Enter data such as the subject of the task, due dates, and the task's priority.

5. From the Status drop-down list, choose the current status of the project: Not Started, In Progress, Completed, Waiting on Someone Else, or Deferred.
6. In the Priority drop-down list, choose Normal, Low, or High priority.
7. In the % Complete text box, type a percentage or use the spinner arrows to enter one.
8. (Optional) To set an alarm to remind you to start the task or complete the task, select the Reminder check box and enter a date and a time in the associated text boxes.
9. Enter any comments, descriptions, or other information related to the task in the comments text box.
10. Click the Categories button and choose a category, or simply enter your own category in the text box.

Access Denied Select the Private check box if you don't want others to see information about your task.

11. Click the Save and Close button when you're finished.

VIEWING TASKS

As in any Outlook folder, you can change how you view tasks in the list using the Current View drop-down list in the Standard toolbar. By default, the Tasks folder displays tasks in a Simple List view. Following is a description of the views you can use to display the Tasks folder:

- **Simple List** Lists the tasks, completed check box, subject, and due date.
- **Detailed List** Displays the tasks, priority, subject, status, percent complete, and categories.
- **Active Tasks** Displays the same information as the detailed list but doesn't show any completed tasks.
- **Next Seven Days** Displays only those tasks you've scheduled for the next seven days, including completed tasks.
- **Overdue Tasks** Shows a list of tasks that are past due.
- **By Category** Displays tasks by category; click the button representing the category you want to view.
- **Assignment** Lists tasks assigned to you by others.
- **By Person Responsible** Lists tasks grouped by the person who assigned the tasks.
- **Completed Tasks** Lists only those tasks completed, along with their due dates and completion dates.
- **Task Timeline** Uses the Timeline view to display tasks by day, week, or month. Figure 16.2 shows the tasks assigned within one week.

Save What Settings? Depending on the changes you make to a view, Outlook might display the Save View Settings dialog box asking if you want to save the view settings before you switch to a different view. Generally, you'll want to discard the Current View settings and leave everything the way you found it.

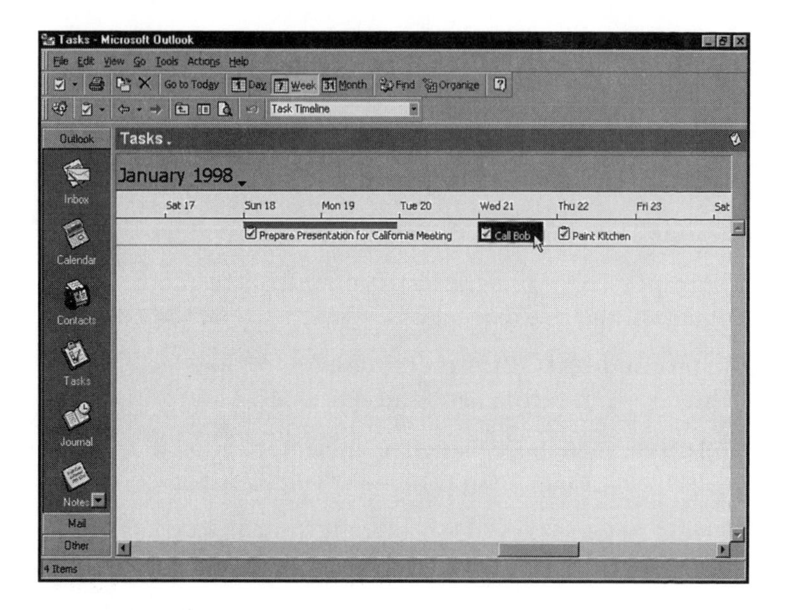

FIGURE 16.2 Double-click a task in Timeline view to edit it.

MANAGING TASKS

When working with a task list, you can add and delete tasks, mark tasks as completed, and arrange the tasks within the list. You also can perform any of these procedures in most of the task views described in the previous section. For information about printing a task list, see Lesson 19, "Printing in Outlook."

Figure 16.3 shows the Tasks folder; the following list describes how to manage certain tasks in the list.

- To quickly add a task, click the top row of the task list where it says "Click Here to Add a New Task" and enter the subject and date.
- To edit a task, double-click the task in the list. The task dialog box appears.

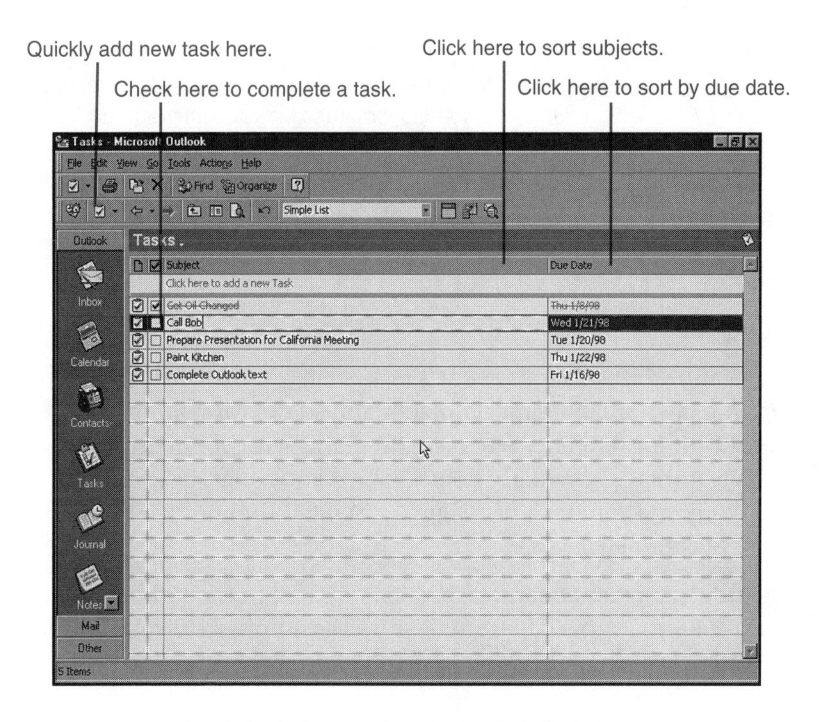

FIGURE 16.3 Add, delete, and sort the tasks in your list.

- To mark a task as completed, click the check box in the second column from the left, or right-click the task and choose Mark Complete from the shortcut menu. Outlook places a line through the task.
- To delete a task, right-click the task and choose Delete from the shortcut menu.
- To assign a task to someone else, right-click the task and choose Assign Task from the shortcut menu. Fill in the name of the person to whom you want to assign the task, and click the Send button to email him or her the task request.
- To assign a new task to someone else, choose Tasks, New Task Request. Create the task as you normally would, but send the task as an email by clicking the Send button.

Get Rid of the Default Task If you don't want to leave the Start Up Microsoft Outlook task on your list, you can right-click the task and choose Delete.

RECORDING STATISTICS ABOUT A TASK

You can record statistics about a task, such as time spent completing the task, billable time, contacts, and so on, for your own records or for reference when sharing tasks with your coworkers. This feature is particularly helpful when you assign tasks to others; you can keep track of assigned tasks and find out when they're completed.

To enter statistics about a task, open any task in the task list and click the Details tab. Figure 16.4 shows a completed Details tab for a sample task.

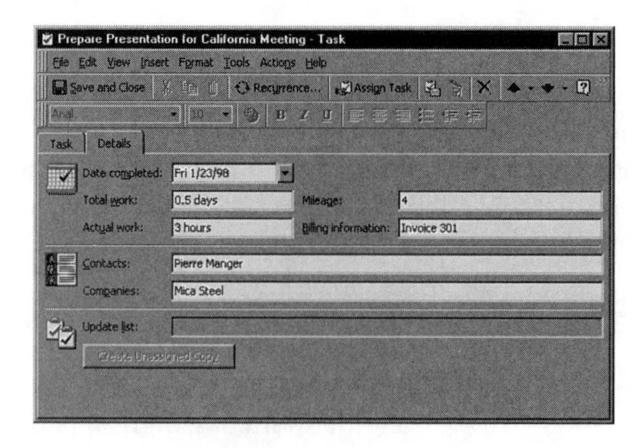

FIGURE 16.4 Fill in the status of the task so you can share it with others and keep personal records.

You can export task lists and other Outlook information to a variety of applications, such as Microsoft Excel. Click File, then Import and Export. A Wizard will walk you through the steps so that you can place the appropriate task information in the cells of a spreadsheet or in a document in a word processor.

The following list describes the text boxes in the Details tab and the types of information you can enter:

- **Date Completed** Enter the date the task was completed, or click the arrow to display the calendar and choose the date.
- **Total Work** Enter the amount of time you expect the task to take. When you complete the job, Outlook calculates the actual time spent and enters it in this text box.
- **Actual Work** Enter the amount of time it actually took to complete the job.
- **Mileage** Enter the number of miles you traveled to complete the task.
- **Billing Information** Enter any specific billing information, such as hours billed, resources used, charges for equipment, and so on.
- **Contacts** Enter the names of in-house or outside contacts associated with the task. Separate multiple names with semicolons.
- **Companies** Enter the names of any companies associated with the contacts or with the project in general. Use semicolons to separate multiple names.
- **Update List** Automatically lists the people whose task lists are updated when you make a change to your task.
- **Create Unassigned Copy** Copies the task so it can be reassigned; use the button to send a task to someone other than an original recipient.

To track tasks you've assigned to others and to receive status reports, follow these steps:

1. On the Tools menu, click Options; the Options dialog box appears. Click the Other tab, and then click Advanced Options.
2. In the Advanced Options dialog box, click Delegated Tasks. The Delegated Tasks dialog box opens.
3. To automatically track the progress of new tasks you assign to others, select the Keep Updated Copies Of Assigned Tasks On My Task List check box.
4. To automatically receive notification when an assigned task is complete, select the Send Status Reports When Assigned Tasks Are Completed check box.
5. After you've made your selections, click OK in each of the three open dialog boxes to return to the Outlook window.

Color Your Task List You can also set color options for overdue and completed tasks. Click the Task Options button on the Preferences tab of the Outlook Options dialog box.

In this lesson, you learned to enter a task and record statistics about the task. In the next lesson, you learn to use the Journal.

Using the Journal

LESSON 17

In this lesson, you learn to create journal entries manually and automatically and to change views in the Journal.

Creating a Journal Entry

You can create a record of various items and documents so you can track your work, communications, reports, and so on. In the journal, you can manually record any activities, items, or tasks you want. You also can automatically record email messages, faxes, meeting requests, meeting responses, task requests, and task responses. Additionally, you can automatically record documents created in the other Office applications: Access, Excel, Office Binder, PowerPoint, and Word.

Journal A folder within Outlook that you can use to record interactions, phone calls, message responses, and other activities important to your work.

Item An article or object in Outlook, such as a task, appointment, or contact.

You can automatically or manually record items in your journal. You can, for example, choose to automatically record your email messages, meeting requests, task responses, and so on. When you automatically record items in the journal, Outlook records all items you receive. However, if you don't want to record all items, you can have Outlook record only those items you choose by manually adding them to your journal. For example, you might add only the email relating to one account or one client instead of all email you receive.

RECORDING AN ENTRY MANUALLY

To create a journal entry manually, follow these steps:

1. In the Inbox folder (or any other folder in Outlook), select the item you want to record in the journal and drag it onto the Journal folder in the Outlook Bar. The Journal Entry dialog box appears (see Figure 17.1).

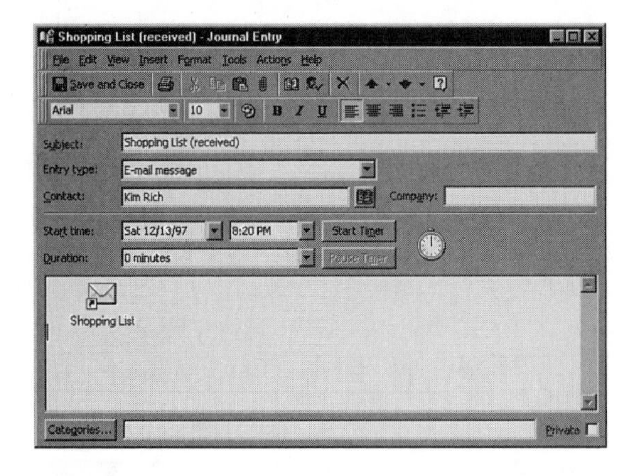

FIGURE 17.1 Drag any item from a folder onto the Journal icon in the Outlook Bar to add the item to the Journal.

2. The information in the Subject, Entry Type, Contact, and Company boxes and some other information is entered for you from the selected task, contact, or other selected item. However, you can change any of the statistics you want by entering new information in the following text boxes:

   - **Subject** Displays the title or name of the item.
   - **Entry Type** Describes the item based on its point of origin, such as a Word document, Meeting or Appointment, and so on.

- **Contact** Lists the name(s) of any attendees, contacts, or other people involved with the selected item.
- **Company** Lists the company or companies associated with the contacts.
- **Start Time** Displays the date and time of the meeting, appointment, or other item.
- **Start Timer** Like a stop watch, the timer records the time that passes until you click the Pause Timer button.
- **Pause Timer** Stops the timer.
- **Duration** Enter the amount of time for completing the item.
- **Text box** Displays a shortcut to the item itself, such as the Calendar appointment, Contact, or Message, that you originally dragged onto the Journal folder. You can open the item by double-clicking the shortcut icon.
- **Categories** Enter or select a category in which to place the item.

3. Click Save and Close to complete the Journal entry.

Time Your Calls When making phone calls or meeting with clients, create a journal entry to record the event, and use the Start Timer and Pause Timer buttons to record billable time.

If you want to create a new journal entry, but you don't have a contact, task, email, or other item that you want to use to create the entry, you can manually record a journal entry by following these steps:

1. Change to the Journal folder.

2. Choose Actions, New Journal Entry or click the New Journal Entry button on the Standard or Advanced toolbar. The Journal Entry dialog box appears.

3. Enter the subject, entry type, contact, time, and any other information you want to record.
4. When you finish, click the Save and Close button.

AUTOMATICALLY RECORDING ENTRIES

You can set options to automatically record items and their related contacts or statistics about Microsoft Office documents you create. Suppose, for example, that you want to keep a record of all memos you send to your boss. You can record them in your journal.

To set the options to automatically record journal entries, follow these steps:

1. In the Journal folder, choose Tools, Options. The Options dialog box appears. Click the Preferences tab if necessary, then click the Journal Options button. The Journal Options dialog box appears, as shown in Figure 17.2.

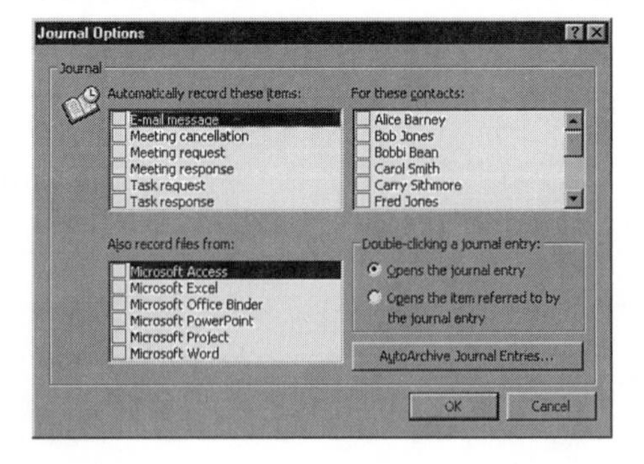

FIGURE 17.2 The Journal Options dialog box is where you set the options for automatically recording items in your Journal.

2. In the Automatically Record These Items list, check those items you want Outlook to automatically record in your journal. (The items recorded correspond with the people selected in the list of contacts in step 3.)

3. In the For These Contacts list, check any contacts you want automatically recorded in the Journal. Outlook records any items checked in step 2 that apply to the selected contacts.
4. In the Also Record Files From list, check the applications for which you want to record journal entries. Outlook records the date and time you create or modify files in the selected program.

Automatic and Easy When you're creating a new contact in Outlook, you can set items to be automatically recorded in the journal by choosing the Journal tab in the Contact dialog box and checking the Automatically Record Journal Entries for This Contact check box.

VIEWING JOURNAL ENTRIES

By default, the Journal folder displays information in the Timeline view and By Type, as shown in Figure 17.3. However, you can display the entries in various views, as described in the following list. To select a particular view, click the Current View drop-down button on the Advanced toolbar.

Save Settings? As in other views, Outlook might display the Save View Settings dialog box to ask if you want to save the view settings before you switch to a different view. You're probably getting used to this dialog box by now.

- **By Type** In Timeline view, this option groups journal entries by type, such as email messages, meetings, Word documents, and so on. Double-click a type to display its contents, and then position the mouse pointer over an entry to view its contents or name.

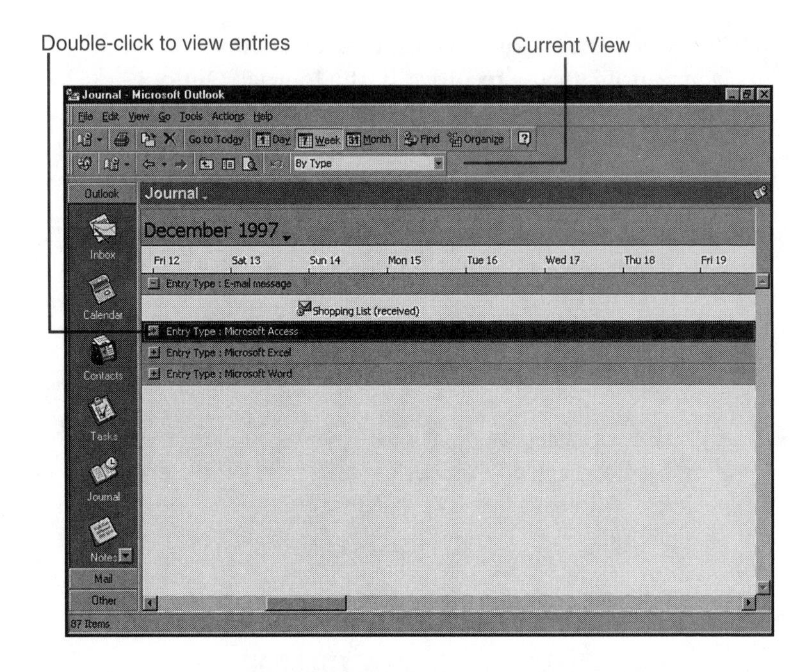

FIGURE 17.3 View the journal entries by type.

Using Journal Options? When you switch to the Journal in the Type view, a Journal Options dialog box appears. This dialog box allows you to specify which email messages will be recorded in the Journal based on the contact they are received from. This dialog box also allows you to select which application use will also be recorded in the Journal, such as Excel, Word, or Access.

- **By Contact** In Timeline view, this displays the name of each contact that you selected in the Options dialog box. Double-click any contact's name to view recorded entries.
- **By Category** If you've assigned categories to your journal entries and other items, you can display your journal entries by category in the Timeline view.

- **Entry List** Displays entries in a table with columns labeled Entry Type, Subject, Start, Duration, Contact, and Categories.
- **Last Seven Days** Displays entries in an entry list, but includes only those entries dated within the last seven days.
- **Phone Calls** Lists all entries that are phone calls.

Sort Journal Entries You can click the heading bar—Subject, Start, or Duration—in any Entry list view to sort the items in that column in ascending or descending order.

In this lesson, you learned to create journal entries manually and automatically and to change views in the Journal. In the next lesson, you learn to create notes.

LESSON 18

Creating Notes

In this lesson, you learn to create, sort, and view notes.

Creating Notes

If you've ever used a paper sticky note to remind yourself of tasks, ideas, or other brief annotations, Outlook's Notes are for you. Notes are similar to paper sticky notes. You can use Notes to write down reminders, names, phone numbers, directions, or anything else you need to remember. In Outlook, all notes are kept in the Notes folder. You'll have to remember to look at the folder so you can view your notes.

The Long and Short of It Notes don't have to be brief. You can enter pages and pages of text if you want. As you type, the page scrolls for you; use the arrow keys and the Page Up/Page Down keys to move through the note text. Keep in mind, however, that the purpose of the note is a quick reminder, or information that you will eventually transfer to one of the other Outlook items, such as an appointment or task.

To create a note, click the Notes folder on the Outlook Bar and then follow these steps:

1. In the Notes folder, choose Actions, New Note or click the New Note button on the Standard or Advanced toolbar. A note appears, ready for you to type your text).
2. Enter the text for your note (see Figure 18.1).

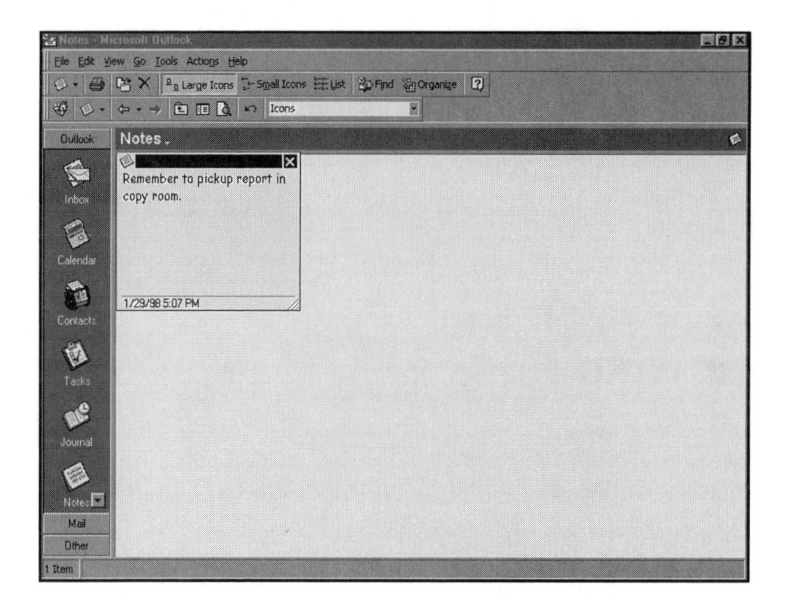

FIGURE 18.1 A note automatically includes the date and time it was created.

3. When you finish, click the Close (X) button to close the note. You can reopen a note and enter as much text or edit text as you need to.

If you press Enter after entering text in the note, you create a line break and you create a title, of sorts, at the same time. Only the text before the hard return displays when the note is closed. If you do not add a hard return, but enter the note text so that it automatically wraps from line to line, the entire note text appears below the note in Icons view.

SETTING NOTE OPTIONS

You can change the default color and size of your notes. You also can change the default font used for your notes. To set note options, follow these steps:

1. In the Notes folder (or any of the Outlook folders), choose Tools, Options. The Options dialog box appears. On the Preferences tab, click Note Options; the Notes Options dialog box appears (see Figure 18.2).

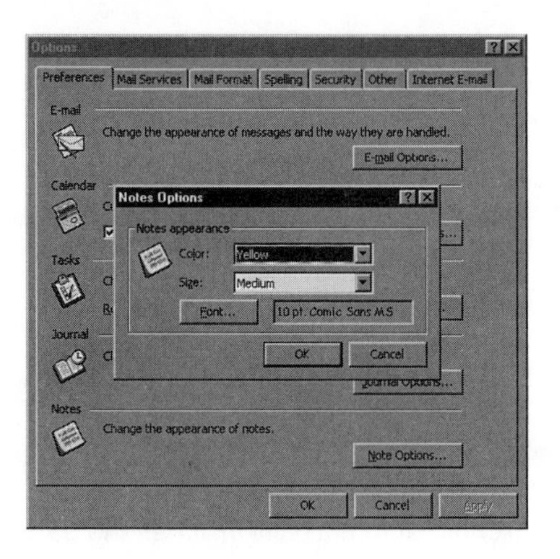

FIGURE 18.2 Customize your notes.

2. The Notes Options dialog box allows you to change the color, size, and font for your notes. Using the Color drop-down box, you can change the color to yellow, blue, green, pink, or white. The default is yellow.

3. Open the Size drop-down list and choose Small, Medium, or Large for the size of the notes. The default is Medium.

4. To change the font, click the Font button. The Font dialog box appears. Change the font, font style, size, color, and other options, and then click OK.

MANAGING INDIVIDUAL NOTES

To open an existing note, double-click it in the Notes folder. You can edit the text in an open note as you would edit any text. To move a note, drag its title bar. You can delete, forward, or print notes; you can change the color of individual notes; and you can specify categories for your notes. You can also drag the notes to the Windows Desktop and arrange them there.

Click an open note's Control menu button to display a menu with the following commands:

- **New Note** Creates a new note but leaves the first note open.
- **Save As** Enables you to save the note and its contents.
- **Delete** Deletes a note and its contents. (You also can delete a note by selecting it in the Notes list and pressing the Delete key.)
- **Forward** Enables you to send the note as an attachment in an email message.
- **Cut, Copy, Paste** Enables you to select text from the note and cut or copy it to the Clipboard. The Paste command enables you to paste items on the Clipboard at the insertion point in the note.
- **Color** Choose another color for the individual note.
- **Categories** Enter or choose a category.
- **Print** Print the contents of the note.
- **Close** Closes the note. (You can also click the Close (X) button in the note's title bar.) A closed note appears in the Notes folder.

VIEWING NOTES

The Notes folder provides various views for organizing and viewing your notes. You can sort notes in any entry list view by right-clicking the heading bar—Subject, Created, Categories, and so on—and selecting the sort method.

The default view is Icons, but you can change the view using the Current View drop-down list in the Standard toolbar. Figure 18.3 shows the Notes folder in the default view.

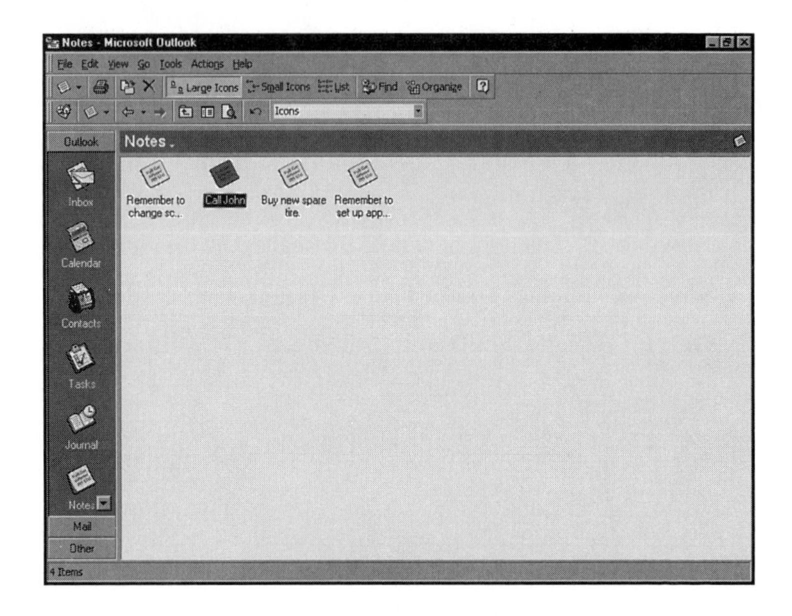

FIGURE 18.3 This view displays the notes in Icons view.

You can choose to display your Notes folder in any of the following views:

- **Icons** Displays the notes as note icons with the message (or a portion of the message) displayed below the icon.
- **Notes List** Displays the notes in a list, showing the title and note contents in the Subject column, the creation date and time, and the categories.
- **Last Seven Days** Displays all notes written in the last seven days, by subject, creation date, and categories.
- **By Category** Displays the categories; double-click a category to show its contents.
- **By Color** Displays notes by their color. Double-click a color to display the notes.

In this lesson, you learned to create, sort, and view notes. In the next lesson, you will learn to print in Outlook.

PRINTING IN OUTLOOK

LESSON 19

In this lesson, you learn to print items in Outlook, change the page setup, preview an item before printing it, and change printer properties.

CHOOSING PAGE SETUP

In Outlook, before you print, you choose the print style you want to use. Each folder—Inbox, Calendar, Contacts, and so on—offers various print styles, and each style displays the data on the page in a different way.

Page In Outlook, this is the area of the paper that will actually be printed on. You might, for example, print two or four pages on a single sheet of paper.

Print Style The combination of paper and page settings that control printed output.

You can choose from Outlook's built-in print styles, modify the default print styles, or create your own print styles. These lists show the default print styles available for each folder. To access the print styles for a particular item, select File, Print. The Inbox, Contacts, and Tasks use the Table style and the Memo style; the Journal and Notes use only the Memo style.

- **Table Style** Displays data in columns and rows on an 8 1/2 by 11 sheet, portrait orientation, 1/2-inch margins.

- **Memo Style** Displays data with a header of information about the message and then straight text on an 8 1/2 by 11 sheet, portrait orientation, 1/2-inch margins.

The Calendar folder provides the Memo style, plus the following styles:

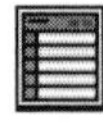

- **Daily Style** Displays one day's appointments on one page on an 8 1/2 by 11 sheet, portrait orientation, 1/2-inch margins.

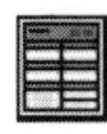

- **Weekly Style** Displays one week's appointments per page on an 8 1/2 by 11 sheet, portrait orientation, 1/2-inch margins.

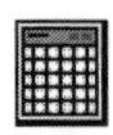

- **Monthly Style** Displays one month's appointments per page on an 8 1/2 by 11 sheet, landscape orientation, 1/2-inch margins.

- **Tri-fold Style** Displays the daily calendar, task list, and weekly calendar on an 8 1/2 by 11 sheet, landscape orientation, 1/2-inch margins.

- **Calendar Details Style** Shows the currently displayed Calendar items and the body text of each item (such as an appointment) in a list format.

The Contacts folder provides the Memo style, plus the following styles:

- **Card Style** Two columns and headings on an 8 1/2 by 11 sheet, portrait orientation, 1/2-inch margins.

- **Small Booklet Style** One-column pages that print the Contacts in a format similar to mailing labels that places multiple Contacts on a page. This style can be printed in Portrait or Landscape modes.

- **Medium Booklet Style** One column that equals 1/4 of a sheet of paper—so that four pages are on one 8 1/2 by 11 sheet of paper, portrait orientation with 1/2-inch margins.

- **Phone Directory Style** One column, 8 1/2 by 11 sheet of paper, portrait orientation with 1/2-inch margins.

Page Setup Only Matters in Printing No matter how you set up your pages, it will not affect your view of tasks, calendars, or other Outlook items onscreen. Page setup only applies to a print job.

You can view, modify, and create new page setups in Outlook. To view or edit a page setup, follow these steps:

1. Change to the folder for which you're setting the page.
2. Choose File, then point at Page Setup. A secondary menu appears that lists the available print types.
3. Select the print type you want to view or edit, and the Page Setup dialog box appears (see Figure 19.1).

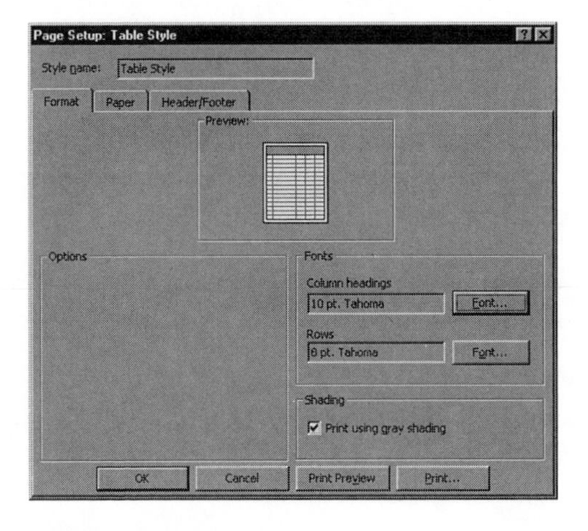

FIGURE 19.1 Customize the print style to suit yourself.

4. Click the Format tab to view or edit the page type, to choose options (in some cases), and to change fonts.
5. Click the Paper tab to view or edit paper size, page size, margins, and orientation.
6. Click the Header/Footer tab to view or edit headers for your pages.

PREVIEWING BEFORE PRINTING

You can choose to preview an item before printing it so you're sure it looks the way you want it to look. If you do not like the way an item looks in preview, you can change the page setup.

Before you display an item in print preview, you must change to the folder containing the item you want to print. Then you can choose to preview the item in any of the following ways:

- Click the Print Preview button in the Page Setup dialog box.
- Choose File, Print Preview.

- Click the Print Preview button on the Advanced Toolbar.
- Click the Preview button in the Print dialog box.

Figure 19.2 shows a calendar and task list in Print Preview. You can change the page setup by clicking the Page Setup button; the Page Setup dialog box appears. Click the Print button to send the job to the printer. Click the Close button to exit Print Preview and return to the Outlook folder.

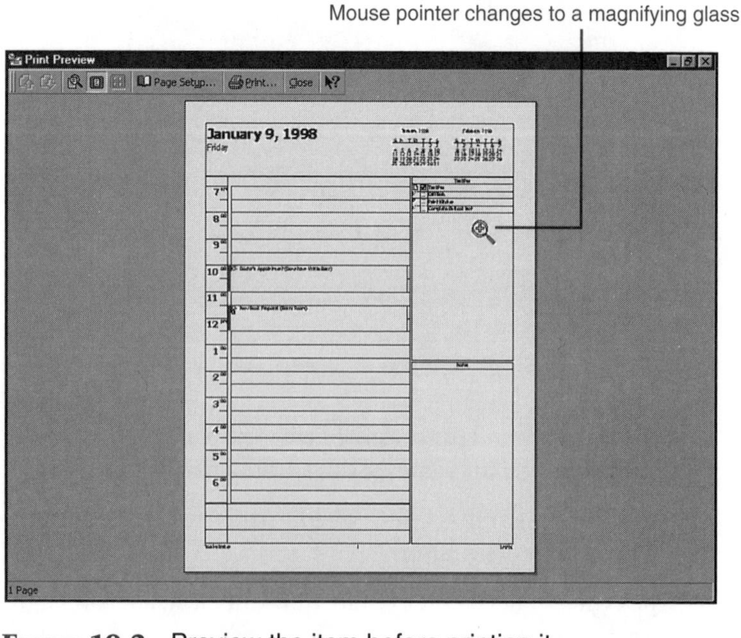

Mouse pointer changes to a magnifying glass

FIGURE 19.2 Preview the item before printing it.

Enlarge the View When the mouse pointer looks like a magnifying glass with a plus sign in it, you can click to enlarge the page. When the mouse pointer looks like a magnifying glass with a minus sign in it, you can click to reduce the view again.

PRINTING ITEMS

After you choose the print style and preview an item to make sure it's what you want, you can print the item. You can indicate the number of copies you want to print, select a printer, change the print style or page setup, and set a print range.

When you're ready to print an item, follow these steps:

1. Choose File, Print or click the Print button on the Standard toolbar. The Print dialog box appears, as shown in Figure 19.3.

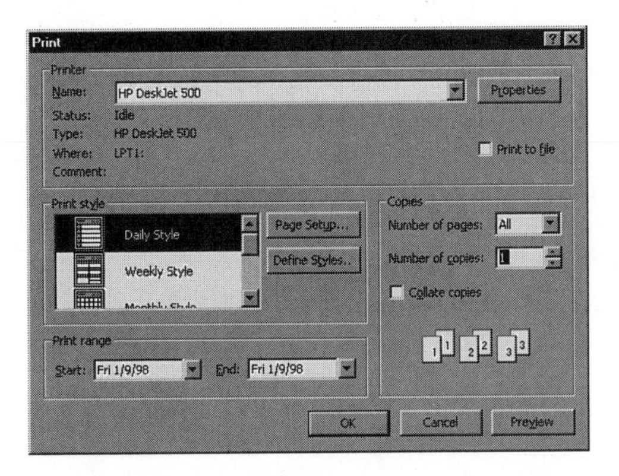

FIGURE 19.3 Set the printing options before printing the item.

2. In the Printer area of the dialog box, choose a different printer from the Name drop-down list if necessary.

3. In the Print Style area, choose a print style from the list. You also can edit the page setup, (with the Page Setup button), edit, or create a new style (with the Define Styles button).
4. In the Copies area of the dialog box, choose All, Even, or Odd in Number of Pages and enter the number of copies you want to print. Click the Collate Copies check box if you want Outlook to automatically assemble multiple copies.
5. Set the print range with the options in that area. (The Print Range options vary depending on the type of item you're printing.)
6. Click OK to print the item.

SETTING PRINTER PROPERTIES

Whether you're printing to a printer connected directly to your computer or to a printer on the network, you can set printer properties. The properties you set apply to all print jobs you send to the printer until you change the properties again.

Printer Properties Configurations specific to a printer connected to your computer or to the network. Printer properties include paper orientation, paper source, graphics settings, fonts, and print quality.

Access Denied? If you cannot change the printer properties to a network printer, it's probably because the network administrator has set the printer's configuration and you're not allowed access to the settings. If you need to change printer properties and cannot access the printer's Properties dialog box, talk to your network administrator.

To set printer properties, open the Print dialog box (by choosing File, Print). In the Printer area, select a printer from the Name drop-down list, and then click the Properties button. The printers' Properties dialog boxes differ depending on the make and model of printer.

Most likely, you'll be able to set paper size, page orientation, and paper source using options on a Paper tab in the dialog box. In addition, you might see a Graphics tab, in which you can set the resolution, intensity, and graphics mode of your printer. A Fonts tab enables you to set options on TrueType fonts, font cartridges, and so on. You might also find a Device Options tab, in which you can set print quality and other options. For more information about your printer, read the documentation that came with it.

In this lesson, you learned to print items in Outlook, change the page setup, preview an item before printing it, and change printer properties. In the next lesson, you learn to manage your files and Outlook items.

LESSON 20

Saving, Opening, and Finding Outlook Items

In this lesson, you learn to save items, open items, and find items in Outlook.

Saving, Opening, and Using Items

Generally, when you finish adding a new task, appointment, meeting, contact, or other item, Outlook automatically saves that item for you or you're prompted to save the item yourself. You can also save most items in Outlook for use in other applications by using the Save As command. After you save an item by naming it, you can open that same item and edit, print, or otherwise use the saved file in Windows applications that support the file type. You might save an item—a journal entry or appointment page, for example—so you can refer to it later, edit the original, or keep it as a record.

Save As When you save an item using the File, Save As command, you can designate a drive, directory, and new filename for that item, as well as a file type.

File Type A file type is the same thing as a file format. When you save a file, you specify a file type that identifies the file as one that can be opened in specific applications. For example, the file extension .DOC identifies a file type that you can open in Word, and the extension .TXT represents a text-only format you can open in nearly any word processor or other application.

Save and Close This command choice is available when you create new contacts, appointments, and tasks. It saves the current item and closes the item's dialog box, returning you to the currently selected folder, such as the Contacts folder or the task list.

To save an item, follow these steps:

1. In the folder containing the item you want to save, choose File, Save As. The Save As dialog box appears (see Figure 20.1).

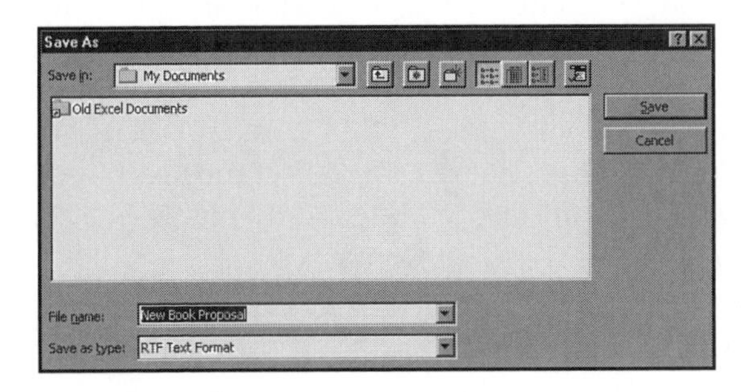

FIGURE 20.1 Save items as files for use in other programs, as copies of the originals, or for later use.

Why Is Save As Dimmed? When the Save As command is dimmed, you must first select an item—an appointment, meeting, task, note, and so on—before you can save it.

2. From the Save In drop-down list, choose the drive to which you want to save the file. From the folders on that drive, select the one you want to save to.
3. In the Save As Type drop-down list, choose a file type. You can save the file in Text Only, RTF Text Format, Outlook Template, and Message Format.

4. After you choose the type, you enter a name for the item in the File Name text box, or accept the default.

5. Click the Save button. Outlook not only lets you save items in different formats, but it also allows you to open certain file formats and use the files in Outlook. The following discussion explains several file formats, including how you would save to the particular file type in Outlook and how you would open a file in this format in Outlook.

   Text Only Saves in ASCII format, which you can use in other applications, such as Word, Notepad, and so on. Save Outlook items in ASCII when you want to send them to someone who does not have Outlook and text-only format will suffice. Any special formatting in the item will be lost when you save in this format. You can also open text-only items in Outlook. Choose File, Open, and then in the Open dialog box, choose Text Only. Select the text file, and then click Open. Information in text-only files can be converted into Messages, Tasks, or Contacts.

   RTF Text Format Saves in rich text format. You can also use this format in Word, Outlook, or Lotus Notes, for example. This format allows you to save items for use in other applications and maintains the text formatting such as bold, underline, and other font attributes.

   To open an RTF file in Outlook or another Windows application, choose File, Open. In the Open dialog box, choose Rich Text Format (or RTF Text Format) in the Files of Type drop-down list. The saved files appear in the file list. Select the file and click the Open button.

   Figure 20.2 shows an email message from Outlook saved as an RTF file and opened in Word. After opening a file, you can format it, cut or copy items to it, insert objects, print, edit, and otherwise manipulate the file. Additionally, you can open the attachment to the email message from within the saved RTF file and read it.

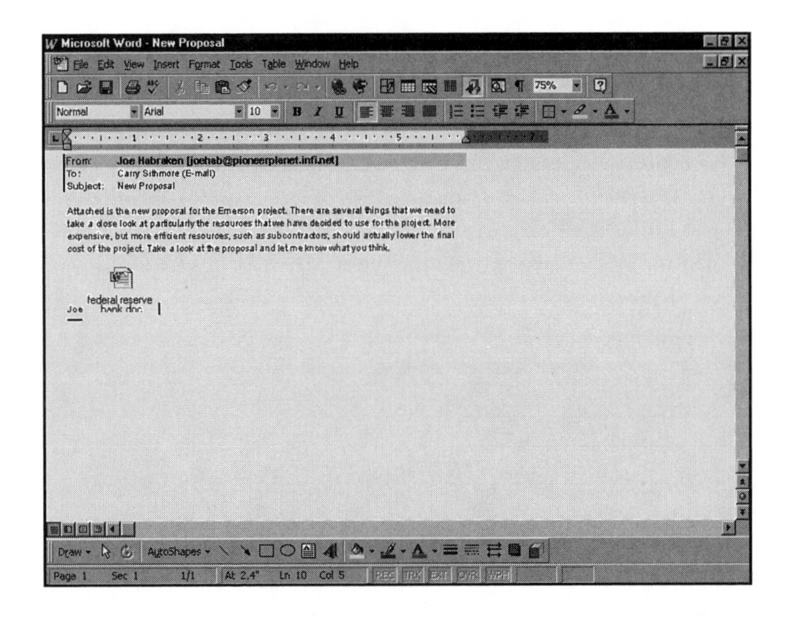

FIGURE 20.2 Exchanging data between applications makes your work easier.

RTF Isn't Listed? If RTF isn't listed in the application's Files of Type list box, see if Text Only is listed. You can also save Outlook items as Text Only.

Outlook Template Saves as a template (or style sheet) that you can use as a basis for other items. You can open an Outlook template when you are in any of the Outlook folders. Templates supply you with ready-made formatting for your Outlook items.

Message Format Saves in a format you can use in your email messages. After you save an item as a message text file, you can insert the item into an email message to send. Suppose you saved a contact's information or an especially long note that you want to share with someone else; you can insert the file as an object into a message and send the email as you normally would. Then the recipient can open the message and the message file.

To insert a message file into a message, open the message and choose Insert, Object. In the Insert Object dialog box, choose Create from File. Enter the path and filename, and click OK. Figure 20.3 shows a message file in the text of an email.

Files As Objects As described in Lesson 11, "Attaching Files, Items, and Objects," you can insert any existing file as an object; therefore, you can insert an RTF, text-only, or message file into a Word document, Excel spreadsheet, mail message, or any other Windows document that supports OLE.

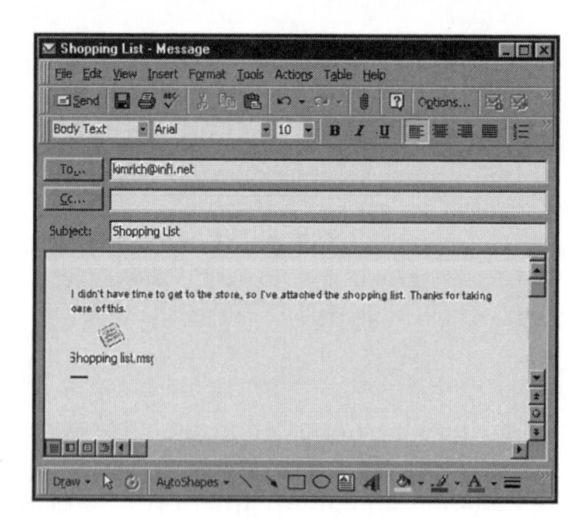

FIGURE 20.3 Open the MSG file by double-clicking its icon.

Use Browse to Find the Object If you don't remember the location and filename of the object you want to insert in your message, use the Browse button in the Object dialog box to locate the file.

FINDING ITEMS

Outlook provides a Find feature that you can use to locate items in your various Outlook folders. You can search for messages, files, journal entries, notes, tasks, contacts, appointments, and so on, depending on which folder you are currently in. When you use the Find feature, it opens in its own pane at the top of the current folder window. You type in a key word or phrase, and the Find feature will search all the items in the current folder for your search word or words. When it finds items that match the search phrase, it will list them in the current folder window. Items not matching the search criteria will be hidden.

Criteria Guidelines you set in the Find dialog box that Outlook uses to find items, such as messages, contacts, or appointments. Included in the criteria you set may be the date an item was created, the title or subject of the item, or specific text within the item.

To find an item in an Outlook folder, follow these steps:

1. Select the folder that you want to search for the item. Choose Tools, Find Items or click the Find Items button on the Standard toolbar. The Find pane appears, as shown in Figure 20.4.
2. Type your search criteria in the Look For box.
3. When you are ready to run the search, click Find Now.
4. The items that match your search word or phrase will appear in the Folder list.
5. You can perform a new search by clicking the Clear Search button; enter a new search phrase in the Look For box and then click Find Now. When you have completed your search, you can close the Find pane by clicking on its Close button.

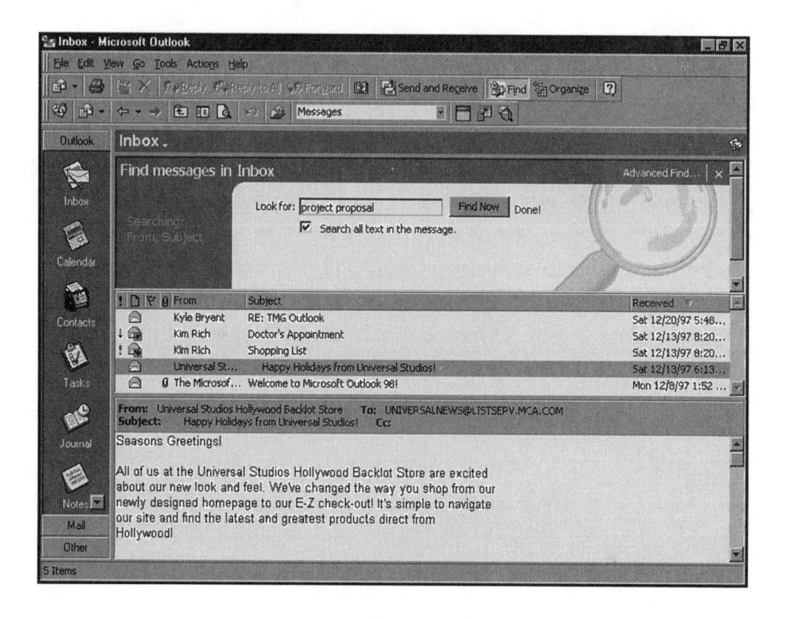

FIGURE 20.4 Use the Find pane to search for items in the current folder.

USING THE ADVANCED FIND FEATURE

The Find pane includes an Advanced Find button in the upper-right corner. You can use Advanced Find to perform more detailed searches than you can with the Find feature. In the Advanced dialog box, you can set multiple search criteria such as a category, from, sent to, and subject (when searching for mail messages, additional search criteria exist for each of the other items found in Outlook).

To use the Advanced Find feature, follow these steps:

1. Open the Find dialog box by choosing Tools, Find Items.
2. Click the Advanced Find button in the upper-right corner of the Find pane.
3. In the Advanced Find dialog box, set the criteria for your search using the criteria boxes found on the various tabs

that appear. For instance, the Message Advanced Find dialog box includes a tab for Messages, More Choices, and Advanced. Each tab provides you with more advanced methods for conducting the search.

4. Set your search conditions on the various tabs. The More Choices tab is the same for each Outlook item and lets you search for items that have not been read or items that have an attachment.

5. When you've finished setting your criteria, click the Find Now button. A box will open at the bottom of the Advanced dialog box that lists the items that have met the search criteria. To open an item, double-click it.

Figure 20.5 shows the Advanced dialog box with the tabs that are used for searching the Inbox or other message folders. A drop-down list at the top left of the dialog box allows you to change the type of item that you are searching.

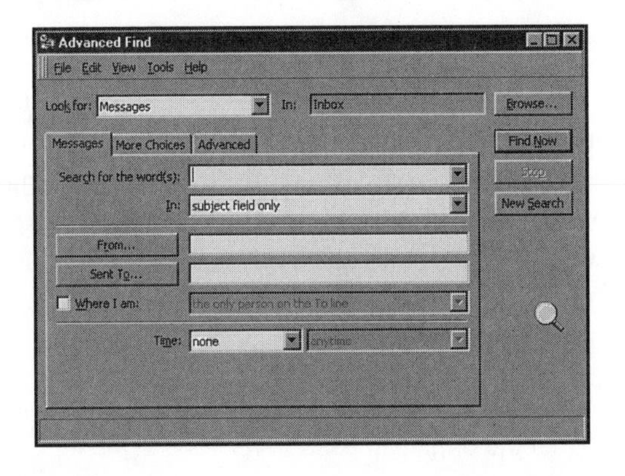

FIGURE 20.5 Set advanced criteria in the Advanced Find dialog box to find specific items.

In this lesson, you learned to save items, open items, and find items in Outlook. In the next lesson, you learn to integrate items between Outlook folders.

USING OUTLOOK INTEGRATION, FORMS, AND TEMPLATES

In this lesson, you learn to use various items in Outlook together (to create a task or an appointment from a mail message and to create a document within Outlook, for example). You are also introduced to the Outlook templates.

CREATING A TASK FROM A MAIL MESSAGE

You can use a mail message to create a task easily in Outlook. Instead of printing the message and then opening your Task List to add the information, you can create the task by using drag-and-drop copying. For more information about using the Tasks folder, see Lesson 16, "Creating a Task List."

You Don't Lose the Message When you use a message to create another item, Outlook copies the message so that the original message remains in the Inbox.

To create a task from a mail message, follow these steps:

1. Open the Inbox folder.
2. Click and drag the unopened mail message from the Inbox window to the Tasks icon on the Outlook Bar. The Task dialog box opens (see Figure 21.1).

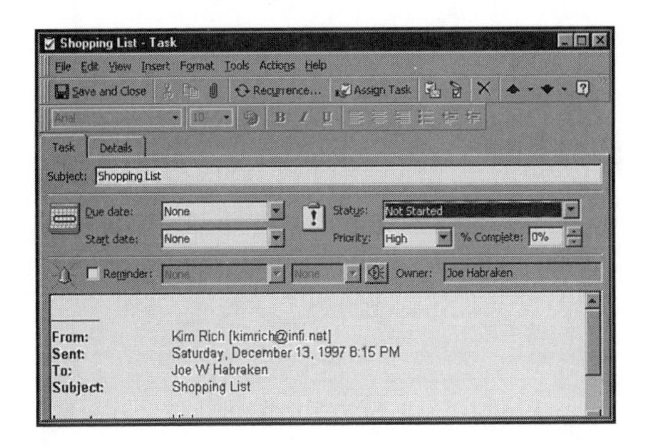

FIGURE 21.1 Create a task from an email message.

3. Change the subject or other data if you want, and then set any options for the task (such as due date, priority, reminders, categories, and so on).

4. Click the Save and Close button, and Outlook adds the task to your list.

CREATING AN APPOINTMENT FROM A MAIL MESSAGE

In addition to creating tasks from messages, you can create an appointment from a mail message. When you create the appointment, you can set a time and date for the appointment, invite attendees to the appointment, create a meeting, and otherwise set options for the appointment. For more information about creating appointments, see Lesson 13, "Using the Calendar."

To create an appointment from a mail message, follow these steps:

1. Open the Inbox and locate the mail message you want to use.

2. Drag the unopened message from the Inbox window to the Calendar folder on the Outlook Bar. The Appointment dialog box opens with some information automatically filled in (see Figure 21.2).

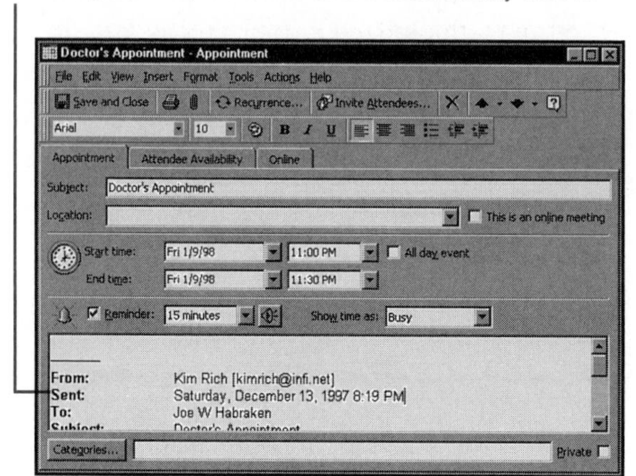

FIGURE 21.2 Create an appointment using the data in a mail message.

3. Add the location to the appointment and make any desired changes in the Subject, Start Time, or End Time boxes, or in any of the other options.
4. Click the Save and Close button to complete the appointment.

CREATE A NOTE FROM ANY ITEM

Just as you can create tasks and appointments from a mail message, you can also create a note from any item in Outlook. Suppose someone emailed you information about a product or service that you want to add to a report; you can simply create a note with the information on it. Or suppose you want to call someone at a certain time later in the day. You can create a note from your contact entry so you won't forget.

You can create a note from a mail message, appointment or meeting, contact, task, or journal entry. After you create the note, you can edit the text in the note without affecting the original item.

To create a note from any Outlook item, drag the item into the Notes folder in the Outlook Bar. Outlook creates and displays the note, and you can edit the text if you want. For more information about notes, see Lesson 18, "Creating Notes."

USING OUTLOOK FORMS AND TEMPLATES

As you already know, Outlook provides you with a number of different forms that you can use to create items for your various Outlook folders; there is an Appointment form, a Contact form, a Journal entry form, and so on. In most cases, you choose a particular form when you are in a particular folder; for instance, when you are in the Calendar folder, you open a new Appointment form.

You can also open the various forms that Outlook provides from the File menu, no matter which folder you are currently in. This means that you can be in the Inbox folder, but you can still quickly open a new appointment form. To open any of Outlook's available forms, select File, then point at New, then select Choose Form. The Choose Form dialog box will appear. Select the form you want to use from the list provided in the dialog box, and then click the Open button.

Outlook also includes a number of templates on which you can base new messages. You can access these templates by using the Choose Form dialog box. The templates offer you alternative layouts and special features such as decorative fonts and graphics to add pizzazz to a new message.

To use an Outlook template for a message, follow these steps:

1. Open the Choose Form dialog box (choose File, New, Choose Form).
2. In the Choose Form dialog box, click the Look In drop-down box arrow and select Templates in File System. The available templates appear in the Choose Form dialog box (see Figure 21.3).

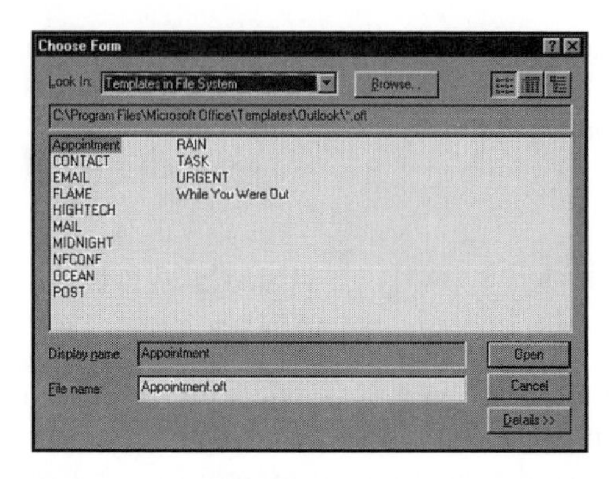

FIGURE 21.3 Base your new message on a specific template in Outlook.

3. Select the template you want to use and click OK. Outlook displays the message window in which you can create your item.

When you use templates for messages, the person who receives the message must have an email client that can view the special graphics and text formatting options offered to you by the template. If you send messages to people who have a text-only email package, you may want to forgo using the templates. Templates, however, are a good way to dress up your other Outlook items, such as tasks or appointments (see Lesson 9, "Creating Mail," for more information on using special mail types, such as HTML).

In this lesson, you learned to use various items in Outlook together—to create a task and an appointment from a mail message and to create a document within Outlook. In the next lesson, you learn to share data with other Office applications.

Sharing Data with Office Applications

In this lesson, you learn to share data between Outlook and other Office applications.

Creating a New Office Document

You can create a new Office document from within Outlook; for example, you can write a letter, write a report, create a spreadsheet, and so on. To create the document, you work in the actual Office application, such as Word, using that application's tools and features. When you save the document, a shortcut saves to Outlook so you can easily open the document at any time.

Outlook 98 and Older Versions of Office Outlook 98 has been designed to fully integrate with the applications in Microsoft Office 97. You may lose functionality and have problems with the integration features if you use Outlook 98 with an earlier version of Office.

To create a new Office document, follow these steps:

1. In the Outlook window, choose File, New, Office Document. The New Office Document dialog box appears, as shown in Figure 22.1.

I Don't See the New Document Dialog Box In order for this dialog box to appear, Office must be installed and you must have at least one Office template located in the Microsoft Office Templates folder.

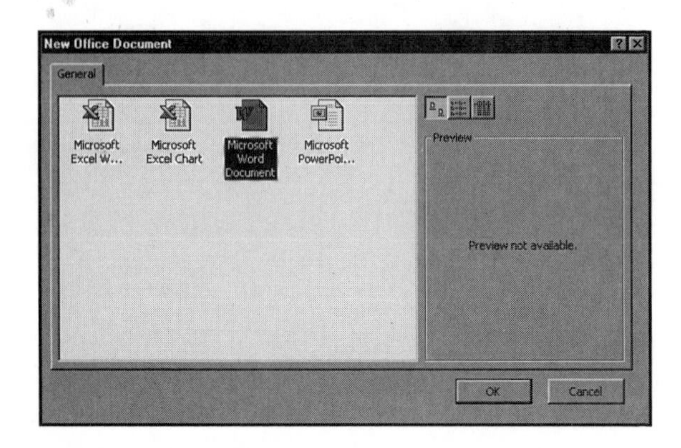

FIGURE 22.1 Select the template that you will base your new Office document on.

2. Select the template for an Excel worksheet or chart, a Word document, or a PowerPoint presentation, and click OK. Select one of the options, and the template opens in a document window. Enter and format the text. Then use the menus to check spelling, create pictures, and otherwise manage the document as you would in a word processor.
3. To print the document, choose File, Print.
4. To save the document, choose File, Save As. The Save As dialog box appears.
5. Enter a filename and file type, and choose a location for the file.
6. Choose File, Close to close the document and the document window. The document is added to the Outlook item you were in when you created it.

To open the document for editing, printing, or other manipulation, double-click it.

CREATING AN OUTLOOK ITEM FROM AN OFFICE FILE

You can create an appointment from a Word document, a mail message from an Excel document, or one of many other items by dragging a file to an Outlook item. This capability is great for when you want to include data in a mail message or record items in your journal. Sharing data between Office applications makes your work easier and more efficient.

To create an Outlook item from an Office file, follow these steps:

1. Open the Windows Explorer window and the Outlook window so you can see both onscreen at the same time (see Figure 22.2).

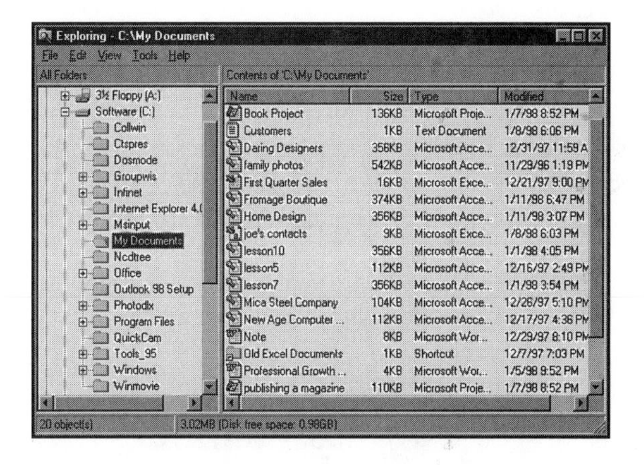

FIGURE 22.2 Arrange the two windows onscreen so you can drag from one to the other.

2. In the Explorer window, select the file from which you want to create an Outlook item, and then drag it to the folder in the Outlook Bar. For example, drag a worksheet to the Task Folder to create a task.

3. The New Item dialog box opens, with the Office file represented as an icon in the item. Enter any details, such as subject, dates, and so on, and then save the item as usual.

Shortcut Drag an Outlook item onto the Windows desktop to create a copy of the item that you can open quickly.

IMPORTING AND EXPORTING FILES

You can import files to Outlook for the other Office applications and export files from Outlook to other Office applications, such as Word and Excel. When you import, you're opening another Office application's file in a format that Outlook can read, so you can use the file's contents in Outlook. When you export, you're saving Outlook data in a format that one of the other Office applications can use.

IMPORTING

You might import files from Access, FoxPro, dBASE, Schedule+, Excel, or some other application for use in Outlook.

To import data, follow these steps:

1. In Outlook, choose File, Import and Export. The Import and Export Wizard appears (see Figure 22.3).

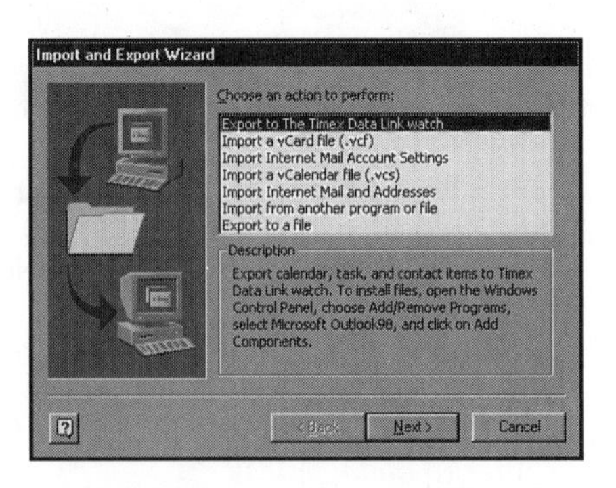

FIGURE 22.3 Import files to use in Outlook.

Wizard In Microsoft Office products, a Wizard is a series of dialog boxes containing instructions and options. A Wizard helps you complete a task.

2. Choose Import from Schedule+ or Another Program or File and click the Next button. The second Wizard dialog box appears.
3. Scroll through the list using the vertical scroll bar if necessary, and choose the type of file you want to import from the list. Click the Next button.

Word's Not There! You won't see Microsoft Word on the list, but you can still import a Word file. Select the Comma Separated Values (Windows) option to import a Word file that you've converted to text-only; first you'll have to use Word to save the Word file in Text Only format. If you are using Microsoft Word as your email editor in Outlook, you can open Word files directly; therefore, Outlook does not include Word on the Import list.

4. In the third Wizard dialog box, enter the path and the filename in the File to Import text box, or click the Browse button and select the file from the Browse dialog box. Set any options in the Options area of the dialog box, and click the Next button.
5. In the fourth Wizard dialog box, select the folder in which you want to import the file, and click Next.

You may wonder why you should go through the import process when you can drag a Word or Excel file into any of the Outlook items. Importing a file translates the imported information into a format that Outlook can use directly. For instance, information imported into a Contact or Task becomes the same as information you entered directly into the Contact or Task. When you drag files onto Outlook items, you are embedding the file in the Outlook item, but you are not converting it. An Excel workbook dragged into the Task Folder is embedded, which means a copy of the workbook becomes a part of the Outlook item. When you double-click an embedded object, such as an Excel Workbook, the Outlook menus and toolbars change to those found in Excel, enabling you to use Excel's features as you work with the embedded object (for more information about Object Linking and Embedding, see the next section in this lesson).

EXPORTING

You can export Outlook files to Access, Excel, Word, and so on for use with other applications. For example, you might export an email message to Word as a memo, or you might export data from your journal into an Excel worksheet. When you export a file, you're saving the file's contents in a format another application can open and use.

To export a file, follow these steps:

1. Select the item you want to export as a file and choose File, Import and Export. The Import and Export Wizard appears.
2. Choose Export to a File and click Next.
3. In the second Wizard dialog box, select the folder to export from and click Next.
4. In the third Wizard dialog box, select the file type, and click Next.
5. In the fourth Wizard dialog box, enter the path and name of the file to be exported, and then click Next.

LINKING AND EMBEDDING OBJECTS

You can use Windows OLE to share data between Office applications. Object Linking and Embedding is a feature that most

Windows applications support. OLE enables you to share data between a source application and a destination application, ensuring that all documents are updated automatically and in a timely fashion. For example, you can link an Excel worksheet to a mail message to ensure that the data you send with the message is up-to-date and accurate. You can also embed objects into mail messages in Outlook.

One of the biggest advantages of using OLE is that you can edit an object by double-clicking it. When you do, the file is updated in both the source and the destination applications with the changes you've made. You can use existing files or create new files for both linking and embedding.

Linking Creating a bridge between two applications so that the data in one application is copied exactly into the second application and updated automatically whenever changes are made.

Embedding Using one application to create an object within another application.

Source The application or document in which the object was created.

Destination The application or document into which the object is copied or embedded.

Object The Word document, Excel worksheet, Outlook Note, or other item that is linked or embedded.

LINKING OBJECTS

Outlook enables you to link data between two or more applications when you want to ensure that all data is kept up-to-date automatically. If, for example, you link an Excel worksheet to an Outlook message, each time you make a change to the numbers in the worksheet, those numbers also change in the linked data in the message.

Linked Files Cannot Be Moved When you create a link between a file, such as an Excel Workbook, and an Outlook item, the link remains in force only as long as the Excel Workbook remains in the same location on your computer. For example, if the Excel Workbook is in an Excel folder on your computer's C: drive, the file must remain in this location if the link with the Outlook item is going to work.

To link an object between Outlook and another application, follow these steps:

1. In Outlook, create a new mail message or reply, and then place the insertion point in the body of the message.
2. Choose Insert, Object. The Insert Object dialog box appears.
3. Choose Create from File. The Insert Object dialog box changes to look like the one shown in Figure 22.4.

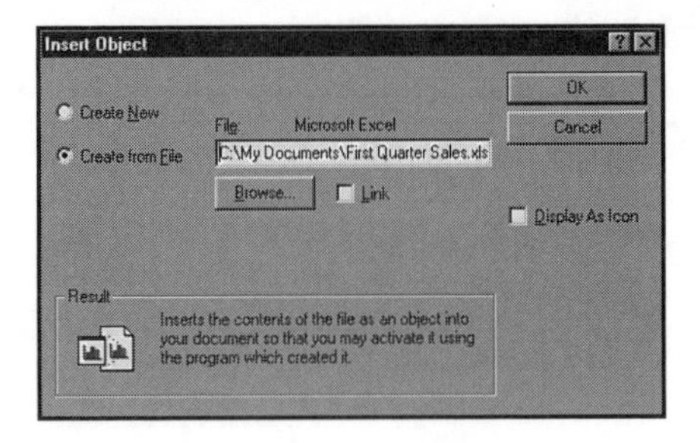

FIGURE 22.4 Create a link to an existing object.

4. Enter the path and filename of the object you want to link in the File text box, or click the Browse button and select the file.
5. Select the Link check box and click OK. Outlook inserts a copy of the object in the message text. The link remains—guaranteeing updated information—until you send the message.

EMBEDDING OBJECTS

You might want to embed a new or existing file, such as a Word table and text, into an email message to send to someone in your company. When you embed the data, the recipient can just double-click the embedded object to open, read, edit, and/or print the file's contents. Note, however, that embedded data (unlike linked data) isn't updated when a source file changes.

To embed an object in Outlook, follow these steps:

1. In Outlook, create a new mail message or reply, and then place the insertion point in the body of the message.
2. Choose Insert, Object. The Object dialog box appears.
3. Choose Create New, and a list of available Object Types appears in the dialog box.
4. Select the object type you want and click OK. Windows inserts a window into the message, from which you can create a document, spreadsheet, chart, or other object.

For example, if you choose to insert a spreadsheet, Windows creates a window within the message that looks like an Excel worksheet. In addition, the Outlook message window changes temporarily to look similar to Excel's, as shown in Figure 22.5.

When you finish entering data, click outside the frame to return to Outlook. At any time, you can double-click anywhere in the frame to edit the data.

Why the Entire Excel Workbook? If you create an object from an existing Excel workbook, Outlook inserts the whole workbook into the item. You can only display one worksheet at a time, however. Double-click the Excel object to choose a different worksheet.

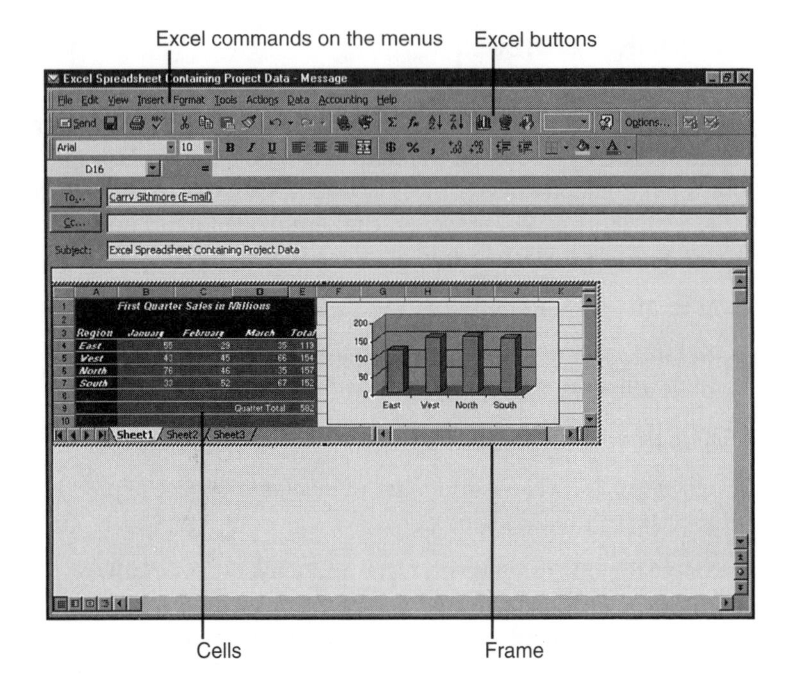

FIGURE 22.5 Create a worksheet from within an Outlook message.

In this lesson, you learned to share data between Outlook and other Office applications. In the next lesson, you learn to archive items.

ARCHIVING ITEMS

LESSON 23

In this lesson, you learn to use AutoArchive and to archive files, retrieve archived files, and delete archived files.

USING AUTOARCHIVE

You can set an option in Outlook to automatically archive your mail messages into files periodically. The AutoArchive feature cleans your Inbox for you but saves the specified messages in an archive file.

Archive To save items to a file that you can open at any time and print, view, or otherwise use. You might, for example, want to archive some of your mail messages to keep for your records instead of leaving those messages in your Inbox. Archived items are removed from the folder and copied to an archive file.

To use AutoArchive, follow these steps:

1. Choose Tools, Options. The Options dialog box appears.
2. Click the Other tab.
3. Click the AutoArchive button to display the AutoArchive options (see Figure 23.1).

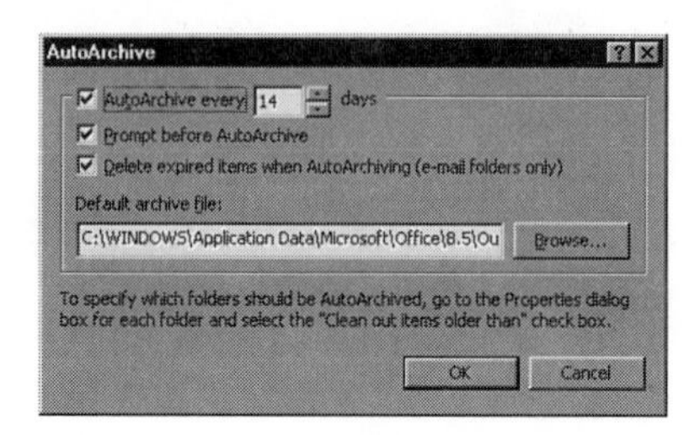

FIGURE 23.1 Specify options for automatically archiving items into files.

4. Choose from the following check box options:

   - AutoArchive Every *x* Days   Enter a number for how often (in days) you want Outlook to automatically archive items. If you enter **14**, for example, when you start Outlook on the fourteenth day, it automatically archives the contents of your folders into an archive file.

   - Prompt Before AutoArchive   If you check this, Outlook displays a dialog box each time it is about to perform the AutoArchive; you can click OK or Cancel to continue or stop the operation.

   - Delete Expired Items When AutoArchiving (E-Mail Folders Only)   Check this box to have Outlook delete messages from the Inbox after archiving them.

5. In the Default Archive File text box, enter a path to where you want to save the file, and name it (if you don't want to use the default).

6. Click OK to close the AutoArchive dialog box. Click OK to close the Options dialog box.

In addition to setting the AutoArchive options in the AutoArchive dialog box, you can set additional AutoArchive options for each folder—Inbox, Tasks, Calendar, and so on. To set an individual folder's AutoArchive options, follow these steps:

1. Right-click the folder in the Outlook Bar to display the shortcut menu.
2. Choose Properties. The item's Properties dialog box appears.
3. Choose the AutoArchive tab. Figure 23.2 shows the Inbox's AutoArchive tab.

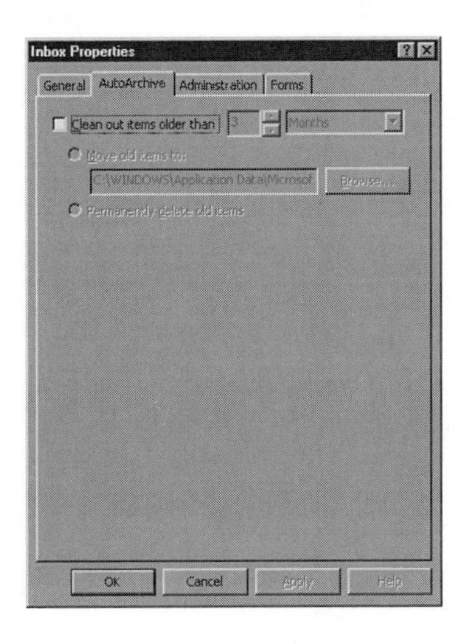

FIGURE 23.2 Set AutoArchive options for individual folders.

4. Set the options you want in the dialog box. You can change the length of time you want the archived files to be saved before they're deleted or saved to another file, and you can enter a path and filename for the second save.
5. Click OK to close the dialog box.

ARCHIVING MANUALLY

You can choose to archive one or two folders or all folders manually whenever you're ready to create an archive file. If you choose to do it yourself, you control exactly how and when archives are created.

To create an archive, follow these steps:

1. Choose File, Archive. The Archive dialog box appears (see Figure 23.3).

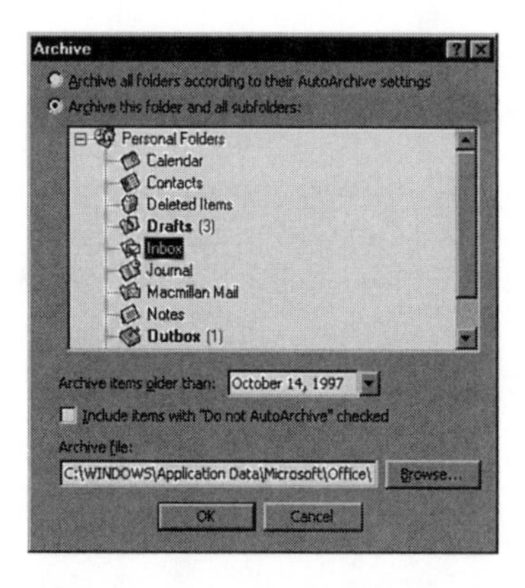

FIGURE 23.3 Enter settings for manual archiving.

2. Choose one of the following options:

   - Archive All Folders According to Their AutoArchive Settings   Use this option to save archives of each folder, using the settings you select in the AutoArchive tab of the folder's Properties dialog box.

   - Archive This Folder and All Subfolders   Select this option to archive the selected folder.

3. Enter a date in the Archive Items Older Than text box, or select a date from the drop-down calendar.

4. In the Archive File text box, enter a path and filename with which to save the file.

5. Click OK to archive the selected folder(s).

RETRIEVING ARCHIVED FILES

You can retrieve an archived file by importing it to the original file. When you retrieve an archived file, it becomes a part of your Outlook folder just as it was before you archived it. Outlook Archived files (.pst files) are saved in a special format and can only be opened using Outlook.

To retrieve an archived file, follow these steps:

1. Choose File, Import and Export. The Import and Export Wizard dialog box appears.
2. Choose Import from Another File or Program and then click Next.
3. On the Import a File screen, select Personal Folders File (*PST) and click the Next button.
4. In the Import Personal Folders dialog box, enter the path and the filename of the archived file. Select any one of the following options, and then click the Next button:
   - Replace Duplicates with Items Imported to overwrite any copies of the data with imported items.
   - Allow Duplicates to Be Created to create duplicates of the items instead of overwriting them.
   - Do Not Import Duplicates to preserve the originals in the folder instead of overwriting them with items from the archived file.
5. In the Choose Folders dialog box of the Import/Export Wizard, choose the folder into which you want to import. (The default is to import the archived item to the Personal Folders area; you may have created subfolders into which you want to import.)
6. Click the Finish button, and Outlook imports the archived files.

DELETING ARCHIVED FILES

The easiest way to delete archived files is by using the Windows Explorer. However, you can also delete files from the Find Files and Folders dialog box or from My Computer (both part of Windows).

To delete an archived file, follow these steps:

1. Open the Windows Explorer and locate the files. Archived files are saved with a .PST extension in the My Documents folder (by default) or any other folder you designate.
2. Open the folder containing the files and select the file(s) you want to delete.
3. Press the Delete key, or drag the file(s) to the Recycle Bin.
4. Empty the Recycle Bin by right-clicking the Bin and choosing Empty Recycle Bin.
5. Close the Explorer by clicking the Close (X) button.

In this lesson, you learned to use AutoArchive and to archive files, retrieve archived files, and delete archived files. In the next lesson, you learn to customize Outlook.

Customizing Outlook

LESSON 24

In this lesson, you learn to set email, calendar, and other options in Outlook.

Setting Outlook Options

You can set all of Outlook's options by using the Options dialog box. (To open the Options dialog box, select Tools, Options.) This dialog box has seven tabs: Preferences, Mail Services, Mail Format, Spelling, Security, Other, and Internet E-mail. Each tab controls a specific category of Outlook's settings. For example, the Other tab, shown in Figure 24.1, controls General options, such as the Deleted Items Folder, AutoArchive, and Preview Pane options.

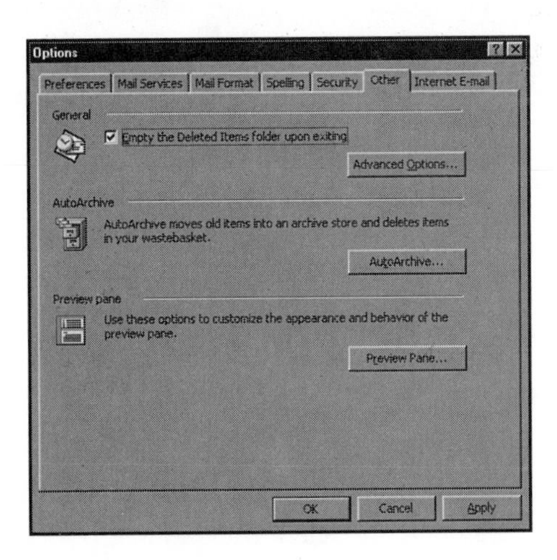

Figure 24.1 The Options dialog box gives you control over all the various features of Outlook 98.

Each tab on the Options dialog box has some obvious settings that you can control with radio buttons or check boxes. Each tab, however, also contains buttons that allow you to set more specific options.

SETTING EMAIL OPTIONS

E-mail, Calendar, Tasks, Journal, and Notes options are set on the Preferences tab of the Options dialog box. To open a more specific dialog box related to the features of each of the Outlook item types, click the appropriate button on the Preferences tab (see Figure 24.2).

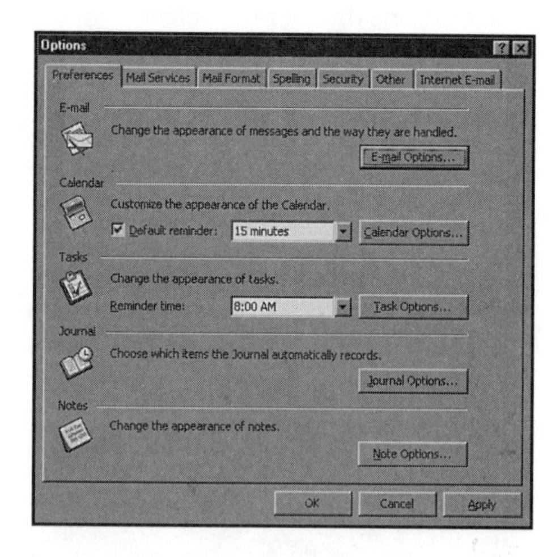

FIGURE 24.2 Customize E-mail, Calendar, Tasks, Journal, and Notes options on the Preferences tab.

To set E-mail options, follow these steps:

1. On the Preferences tab, click the E-mail Options button.
2. The E-mail Options dialog box appears. This dialog box allows you to set items using check boxes and drop-down menus; there are also buttons for Advanced E-mail Options and Tracking Options.

3. In the Message Handling box of the E-mail Options dialog box, check the boxes of the options you want to activate, such as Close Original Message on Reply or Forward or Save Copies of Messages in Sent Items Folder.

4. Two drop-down boxes in the On Replies and Forwards section provide you with options for replying to and forwarding messages. You can choose whether or not you want to include the original message text with replies and forwards, or whether to attach the original message as an attached file.

5. You can also set Advanced E-mail options and Tracking options in this dialog box. When you click the Advanced E-mail Options button, the Advanced E-mail Options dialog box appears, as shown in Figure 24.3. This dialog box allows you to control how unsent messages are handled, what happens when new mail arrives, and the importance level of new messages that you send. When you've completed setting options in this dialog box, click OK.

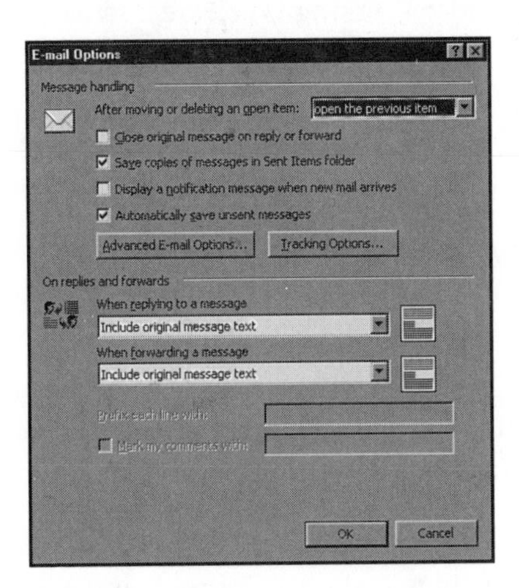

FIGURE 24.3 Advanced E-mail options allow you to control what happens to unsent messages and what happens when new email arrives.

6. The Tracking Options button in the E-mail Options dialog box opens the Tracking Options dialog box. In this box you can set options that notify you when email you send is received and when that email is read. After setting options in this dialog box, click OK. Click OK again to close the E-mail Options dialog box.

SETTING CALENDAR OPTIONS

If you work during unusual days or hours, you can change your default Calendar workweek in the Calendar Options dialog box. Suppose your workweek runs from Tuesday through Saturday, and your workday is from 4 a.m. to 12 noon. You can make changes to the Calendar so that it reflects your actual workweek. You can also set your time zone and add holidays to your calendar. To open the Calendar Options dialog box, click the Calendar Options button on the Preferences tab of the Options dialog box.

Follow these steps to make changes to the Calendar Options:

1. In the Calendar Working Week area, set your starting and ending time (the default is 8 a.m. to 5 p.m.).
2. To set the time zone for your area, click the Time Zone button, and then choose the zone that describes your location.
3. To add holidays to your calendar, click the Add Holidays button. Then check the box representing your country (US is the default) and click OK. Outlook imports the US holidays to the calendar.
4. When you finish setting the options in this dialog box, return to the Preferences tab by clicking OK.

The Preferences tab also allows you to set options for your other Outlook items, such as Tasks, the Journal, and Notes.

SETTING MAIL SERVICES AND MAIL FORMAT OPTIONS

The Mail Services tab allows you to set options that govern which Outlook Profile is loaded when Outlook starts and which of your installed mail services is checked for mail. Click the appropriate check boxes for the services you want checked when new messages, such as faxes and email, are downloaded to your Inbox.

If you installed Outlook for Internet Only, Outlook does not need a profile to load the services that you install such as your Internet email account and Outlook Fax. For more information on the Internet Only and Corporate email installations, see Lesson 3, "Understanding the Outlook Configurations."

Profile A group of settings that control how your mail is delivered, received, and stored in Outlook and the software used to transfer your mail, such as Microsoft Mail, Microsoft Exchange, Lotus Notes, and so on.

Check for New Mail? The mail types listed in the Check for New Mail On list box are added when you add a new profile to Outlook. You add a profile by choosing Tools, Services.

The Mail Format tab in the Options dialog box allows you to choose your Message format, such as HTML, Plain Text, Microsoft Word, and Microsoft Exchange Rich Text. The Mail format that you use will dictate the special fonts and WordMail templates that are available to you. Remember, however, that special fonts and templates will be of no use to you if those receiving your messages do not have email software that can take advantage of the fonts and formatting. To always send plain text to certain individuals, open their Properties dialog box in the Address book and click the Send E-mail Using Plain Text only check box.

Applying Your Changes When you make changes on the tabs of the Options dialog box, you can apply these new options to Outlook by clicking the Apply button. The Options dialog box will remain open, so that you can configure other options.

OTHER OPTIONS DIALOG BOX TABS

The Options dialog box also contains three additional tabs that control other features associated with Outlook. Each tab is listed as follows with a description of the settings available.

- The Spelling tab allows you to change settings associated with Outlook's spell checker. You can choose to have the speller always suggest replacements for misspelled words, always check spelling before sending, and ignore words in uppercase. You can also pick the language of the dictionary.
- The Internet E-mail tab allows you to set the coding scheme for Internet email attachments. Settings are also available that have Outlook check periodically on your network for new email messages.
- The Security tab allows you to set options regarding whether or not outgoing messages should be encrypted or have digital signatures attached to them. There is also an option that allows you to get a digital ID to use for your outgoing messages.

When you complete all the changes you want to make to the Outlook options, click OK to close the Options dialog box.

In this lesson, you learned to set email, calendar, and other options in Outlook. In the next lesson, you learn to use Internet services.

OUTLOOK AND THE INTERNET

LESSON 25

In this lesson, you learn about Outlook and its connection to the Internet, using Outlook Express Newsreader, Microsoft Internet Explorer, and Microsoft NetMeeting.

USING NEWSGROUPS

Microsoft Outlook not only provides all the tools you need to manage your messages, contacts, and calendar, but it also provides you with an easy connection to Internet services, such as newsgroups and the World Wide Web. Outlook even provides you with the ability to conduct real-time meetings over the Internet.

Newsgroups are a large collection of discussion groups held on news servers around the world. A particular newsgroup is much like a bulletin board; you can read messages posted there and post your own. Newsgroups cover information from current events to software, hobbies, pets, and other personal interests.

Newsgroup An Internet online bulletin board that allows users to post and read messages. Newsgroups are part of USENET, which is a consortium of Internet news servers that allow users (such as yourself) to download and post messages.

To access Internet newsgroups and read or reply to the postings there, you need a newsreader. When you install Microsoft Outlook, the Microsoft Outlook Express newsreader software is also installed.

SETTING UP THE NEWSREADER

You can access newsgroups from Outlook by starting the Outlook Express newsreader. First you must make sure that you are connected to the Internet through your corporate network or by your dial-up connection to your Internet service provider. After you've connected, take the following steps to start the Outlook Express Newsreader and download newsgroup postings:

1. In the Outlook window, click the Go menu, and then click News. The Outlook Express Newsreader will open.
2. The first time you use the Newsreader, it will run the Internet Connection Wizard, which leads you through the process of setting up your news server and creating a newsgroup account for yourself. The first screen asks you to type the name you will use when you post messages to your news server (see figure 25.1). After typing a name, click Next.

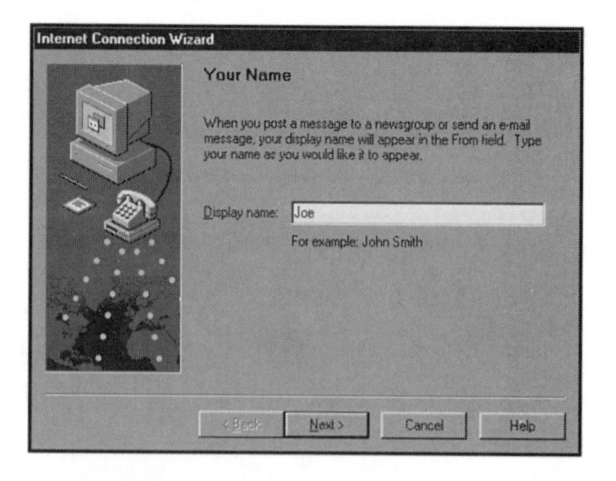

FIGURE 25.1 The Internet Connection Wizard walks you through the steps of setting up your news server.

3. The next screen asks you to provide your email address. Click Next after doing so.
4. On the next screen, you must provide the name of your news server. This name should be provided to you by

your network administrator or Internet service provider. Click Next after entering the server name (it will be something like **news.company.com**).

5. The next screen asks you to type a friendly name for the new account. Type a name and then click Next. The last screen asks you to select the type of connection you will use to access the Internet: your phone line, Local Area Network, or a manual connection. Select the connection type, and then click Next. The last screen appears, letting you know you've completed the process. Click Finish.

Friendly Names for Accounts The friendly name that you choose for your new account in step 5 will appear on your Outlook Express folder list and can be used to open the newsgroups that you subscribe to. This account name differs from the name that you must choose in step 2, which actually identifies the postings that you place on the news server. This name is seen by everyone who looks at the posts in the Newsgroup. You should choose your newsgroup posting name carefully. You don't want to inadvertently offend anyone when you post or have your posts be taken less seriously than you intended.

When you complete the account creation process, the Newsgroups dialog box appears and the newsgroups on your news server are downloaded. Scroll through the list provided and select the newsgroups you want to subscribe to. Click the Subscribe button when appropriate (see Figure 25.2). When you "subscribe" to a particular newsgroup, it will appear as a subfolder of your Newsgroup account in the Outlook Express Folder list. Subscribe to a list when you want to access the posts in it on a regular basis.

After subscribing to the newsgroups you want to read, click the OK button. You return to the Outlook Express window (see Figure 25.3).

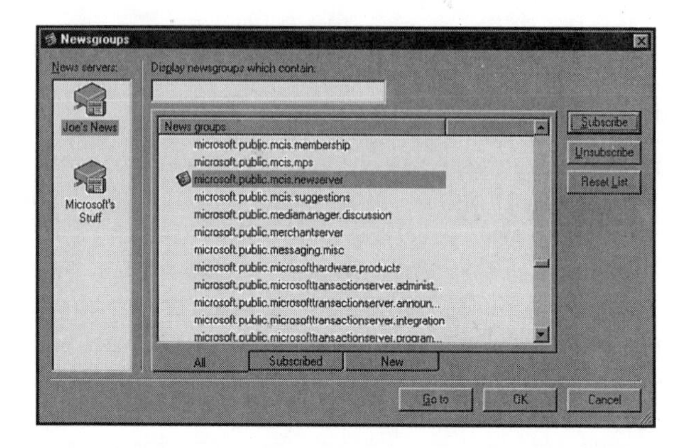

FIGURE 25.2 You can subscribe to the newsgroups that you want to read and post to.

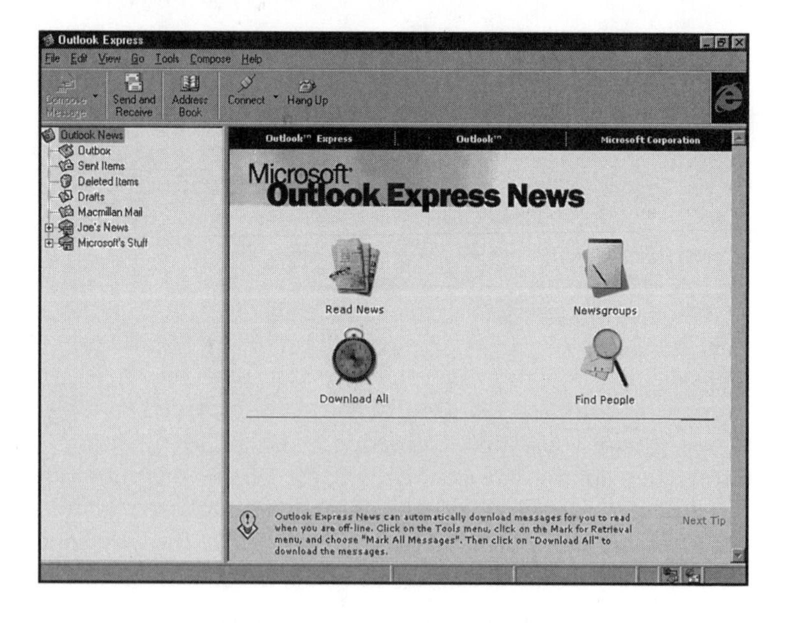

FIGURE 25.3 The Outlook Express Newsreader allows you to read and post messages in Internet newsgroups.

READING NEWSGROUP POSTINGS

After you have set up an account and downloaded and subscribed to newsgroups, you are ready to read and post messages. To read newsgroup postings, click Read News.

The newsgroups that you are subscribed to appear in the Message pane of the Outlook Express window. To view messages in a particular newsgroup, double-click the newsgroup.

Messages in the newsgroup will appear in the Message pane. To read a particular message, click the message. The message text will appear in the preview pane. You can also open a separate message window by double-clicking a particular posting (see Figure 25.4).

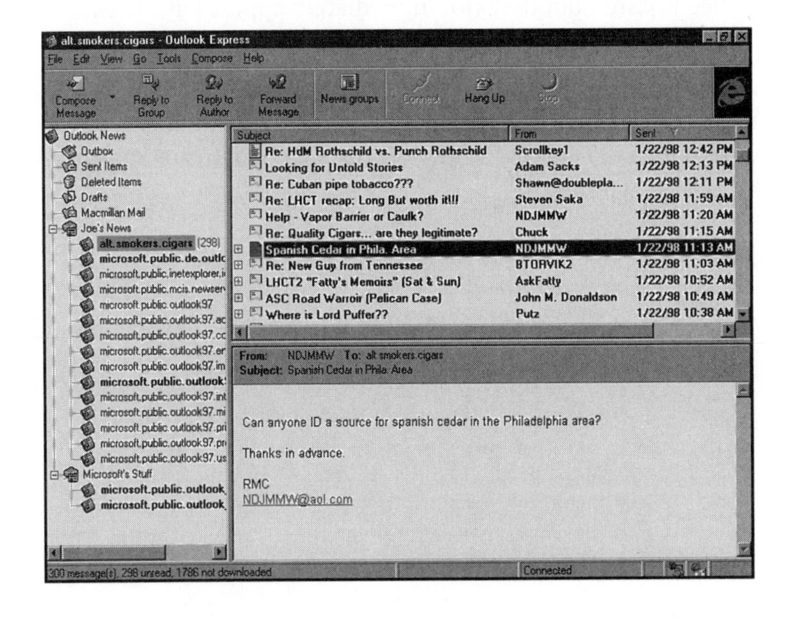

FIGURE 25.4 Select a message in the Newsgroup window to read it in the preview pane.

POSTING TO NEWSGROUPS

To post your own message to a newsgroup, you will follow a procedure that is similar to sending new email messages using Outlook itself. In the Outlook Express window, select the newsgroup you want to post to.

Click the New Message button on the Outlook Express toolbar. A new message window opens. Type a subject for the message in the Subject box. Type the message itself in the message pane of the new message window. After you've completed your message, click the Post button.

A message window will appear telling you that your new message has been posted but may not immediately appear with the messages already in the newsgroup.

When you have completed reading and sending newsgroup messages, you can close the Outlook Express Newsreader. Click the Outlook Express Close (X) button. You will be returned to the Outlook 98 window.

Posting Etiquette When you post to newsgroups, you should follow the same rules of politeness that you use when you converse with someone in person or send email to colleagues and friends. Do not type in all caps; this is considered shouting. Remember that humor and sarcasm are not always apparent in written communication. Be as straightforward and clear as you can in your postings. An extremely annoying post can lead to *flaming*, or a barrage of angry and unsolicited email.

When you do find a post that you want to respond to, or you want to send email to the individual who made the post, select the post message in the Outlook Express message window. Then either click the Reply to Group button (this sends a post in response to the selected post), or the Reply to Author button to send email to the author of the post.

LAUNCHING INTERNET EXPLORER

You can also launch Microsoft Internet Explorer 4 from the Outlook 98 window. This enables you to quickly browse the World Wide Web. Again, before launching Internet Explorer, you must be connected to the Internet either by your company network or by dial-up connection to your Internet service provider.

Launching Other Web Browsers If you use another Web browser, such as Netscape Navigator, you will not be able to launch it directly from Outlook. Create a shortcut for your browser on the desktop so that you can launch it quickly when you need it.

1. To start Internet Explorer, click the Go menu, and then click Web Browser. The Internet Explorer window opens (see Figure 25.5).
2. You can browse the Web using all the features of Internet Explorer. Use links on your home page to move to other Web pages, or click the Search button to find other sites of interest.

Launching Internet Explorer from Outlook Messages You can also launch Internet Explorer from Outlook messages that contain Web page references. Web page addresses in your Outlook email messages appear in blue and serve as hyperlinks. Click the Web address in the message (such as **http://www.mcp.com**), and Internet Explorer will start and open the designated Web page.

When you have completed your use of Internet Explorer, click the Close (X) button in the Explorer window. You will be returned to the Outlook 98 window.

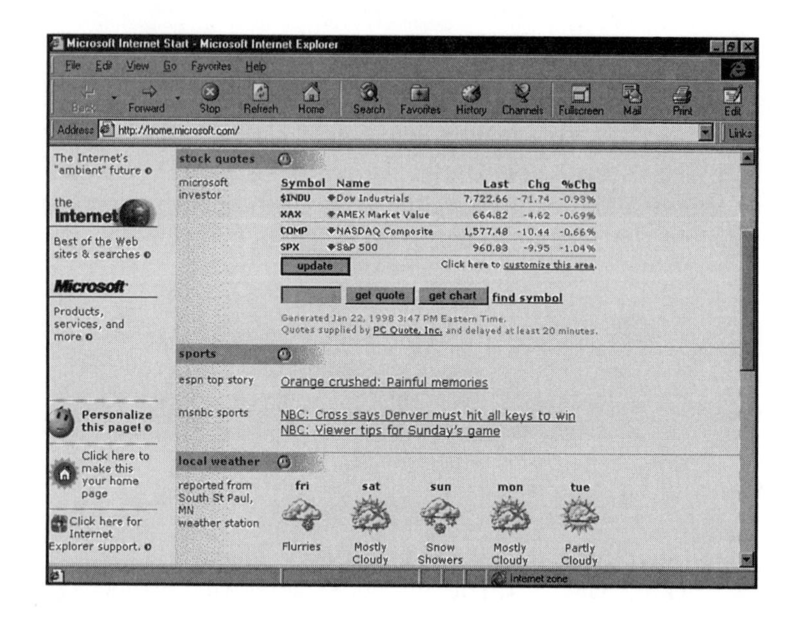

FIGURE 25.5 Internet Explorer provides you with all the capabilities you need to take advantage of the World Wide Web.

LAUNCHING MICROSOFT NETMEETING

Another software package that takes advantage of communication on the Internet and that can be launched from Outlook is Microsoft NetMeeting. Microsoft NetMeeting allows real-time voice and video communication over the Internet. This allows you to conduct "live" meetings without leaving your office.

To start NetMeeting from Outlook, follow these steps:

1. Click Go, and then point at Internet Call; click From Address Book or Start NetMeeting.

2. If you chose the Address Book option, double-click the name of the person you want to hold the meeting with in the Address Book window. NetMeeting will start and connect you to the other participant (skip to step 4). If you clicked Start NetMeeting, you will have to select the other participant from the list of users currently logged in to the NetMeeting server, as shown in Figure 25.6.

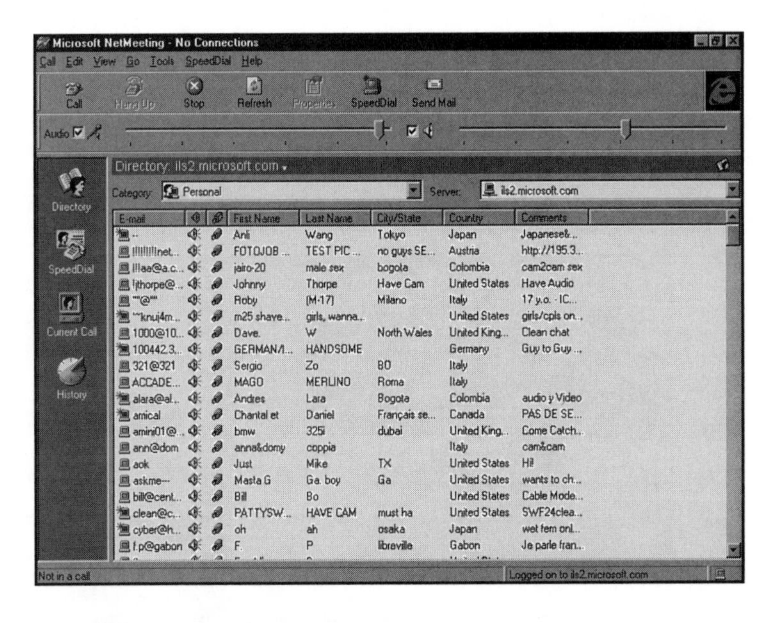

FIGURE 25.6 The NetMeeting server listing provides a list of all individuals currently logged in to the various Microsoft NetMeeting communication servers.

Launching NetMeeting from Outlook If you plan to launch NetMeeting sessions directly from the Address Book or your Contacts list, you must make sure that you have entered the contact's email address in the appropriate field. NetMeeting uses the email address to find the person on the NetMeeting Server that she is connected to.

3. Double-click the name of the person you want to meet with in the NetMeeting directory server list.

4. Regardless of which route you used to start the new meeting, the Current Call window will open. At this point you are connected to the other individual and can hold your meeting using audio and video (if the appropriate hardware is available on both users' computers). NetMeeting

also provides a Chat window that the participants can use to communicate by typing (see Figure 25.7).

5. When you have completed your meeting, close the Current Call window, and then close the NetMeeting window. You will be returned to the Outlook 98 window.

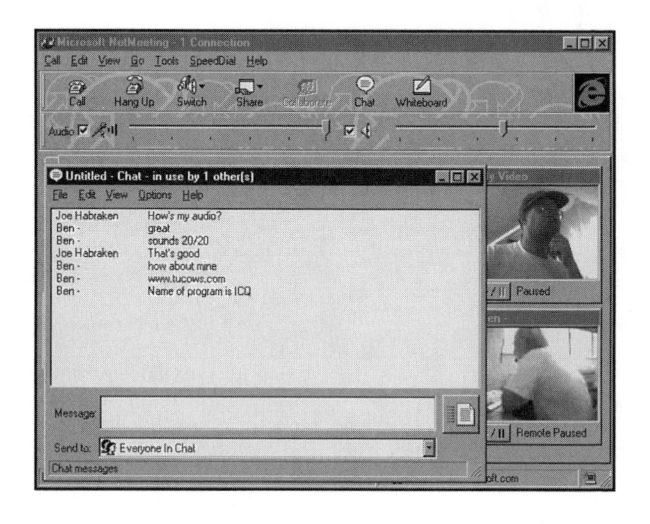

FIGURE 25.7 NetMeeting's Current Call window allows you to communicate with others using audio, video, or your keyboard.

Launching NetMeeting from the Contacts Folder
You can also launch NetMeeting conferences from your Contacts folder. Open a Contact form for a particular contact. Click the Actions menu, then click Call Using NetMeeting. NetMeeting will be launched, and you will be connected to the appropriate meeting server and then to your contact.

In this lesson, you learned how to read newsgroup postings using the Microsoft Outlook Express newsreader. You also learned to launch Internet Explorer from the Outlook window and to launch meetings on the Internet using Microsoft NetMeeting.

INDEX

A

B-C

D

E

F

G-H

I

J-K

L-M

N

O

P

Q-R

S

T

U-V

W-Z